George Albert Cooke

The History and Song of Deborah

Judges IV and V

George Albert Cooke

The History and Song of Deborah
Judges IV and V

ISBN/EAN: 9783337232443

Printed in Europe, USA, Canada, Australia, Japan

Cover: Foto ©Lupo / pixelio.de

More available books at **www.hansebooks.com**

THE

HISTORY AND SONG OF DEBORAH

JUDGES IV AND V

BY THE

REV. G. A. COOKE, M.A.

HEBREW LECTURER AT ST. JOHN'S AND WADHAM COLLEGES, OXFORD

Oxford

HORACE HART, PRINTER TO THE UNIVERSITY

1892

[*Privately printed*]

CORRIGENDA ET ADDENDA.

—•—

Page 3, line 2 from bottom, *for* New Series *read* New Series, vol. v.
,, 15 ,, 1 ,, ,, Well. ,, Wellh.
,, 17 ,, 11 ,, ,, Jéhovists ,, Jéhovistes.
,, 24 ,, 13 ,, ,, ptcp. ,, participial adjective.
,, 34 ,, 17 ,, ,, שִׂי ,, שִׂי
,, 47 ,, 18 from top ,, 2 C. 35, 32 ,, 2 C. 35, 22.
,, 57 ,, 8 ,, ,, Ex. 17, 8 ,, Ex. 17, 8 ff.

Page 10, line 6. Ps. 83, 10. 11 implies the same situation. It places the overthrow at Endor, the modern Endūr, at the foot of Tabor. Baed. p. 245. The mention of Jabin and Sisera in the Ps. presupposes the union of the two traditions : see p. 17.

Page 36, on לָהֶם. The accent perhaps rather shews that the Mass. understood the word as an unusual form of לָחֶם (cf. פֶּלֶט) : Stade, § 88, 3.

Page 37, line 19 from bottom. Field wrote in 1875. Wellh. (Bleek, *Einl.* iv. aufl. 1878, p. 592) attributes the same explanation to Ewald, *Gött. G. A.* 1867, pp. 635 ff. Possibly each made it independently.

Page 39, line 19 from top. Another emendation that has been suggested is שירו.

Page 43, line 8 from bottom. Perhaps עממים was the north Palestinian form : it is the usual one in Aramaic.

Page 45, line 2 from top. פְּלַגּוֹת may come either from a sing. פְּלַג, in which case the proper parallel would be מֵעַט, מְעַטִּים, or more probably from a sing. פְּלַגָּה, פְּלַג like קָטָן קְטַנָּה, קְטַנּוֹת. But the punctuation is anomalous, and perhaps we should read פְּלַגּוֹת from פְּלַגָּה.

Page 50, on הלמות. The ending וּת is very strange in a noun denoting a concrete object ; the only parallel seems to be חַלָּמוּת *purslain* in Job 6, 6. Nouns ending in וּת from verbs ל"ה sometimes have a concrete sense (רְמוּת, גָּלוּת, כְּסוּת); but probably in these cases the termination is not וּת but simply ת, the ו representing the original 3rd radical. See Barth, *Die nominalbildung in den Sem. sprachen*, 1891, ii. pp. 411 ff. At any rate the form here is open to doubt.

THE HISTORY AND SONG OF
DEBORAH : JUDGES IV. AND V.

PART I.

THE HISTORY.

THE story of Deborah and Barak is told in two versions,
the one in prose and the other in poetry. Of these, the
latter possesses the high authority of a document beyond
doubt contemporary with the events it describes. All
critics are agreed upon the antiquity of the poetical version;
indeed there is nothing in the Old Testament of the same
extent and integrity which can be placed earlier. The style
and language, equally with the subject-matter, belong to an
archaic age; the religious temper and the political situation are both those of the period of the Judges; and the
whole song glows with the passionate enthusiasm of a
poet who was keenly interested, and perhaps took part, in
the heroic deeds of which he sings [1]. The antiquity of the
poem, then, may be taken for granted, and its value as
historical evidence must be admitted at the same time. But
we have another authority at our disposal, the corresponding
narrative in *ch.* 4. We must examine the contents and
character of this version before we can use it for the purpose

---

[1] 'Hoc mihi videtur gravissimum argumentum, canticum Deborae statim
post rem gestam ortum esse, quod in carmine nostro plus historiae continetur,
quam in ipsa descriptione historica.' Böttger in Käuffer's *Studien der säch-
sischen Geistlichen*, Dresden, 1842, quoted by Hilliger. Wellhausen, *Die Composition des Hexateuchs u. s. w.*, 1889, p. 223 *n.*, notes as evidence for this, the
fact that the number of warriors in Israel is reckoned at 40,000 men (in Pent.
600,000) *v.* 8, the wild passion of *vv.* 25-27, and the exultation over the
disappointment of Sisera's mother *vv.* 28 ff.

of gaining as consistent an idea as the circumstances will allow of the actual course of events. We shall find that *ch.* 4 is clearly of later date, and therefore of less historical value, than *ch.* 5, which, of course, will be our criterion. Our method, then, will be to test the internal evidence afforded by *ch.* 4, exhibiting the difficulties which it presents, and then to compare the narrative with the external evidence contained in *ch.* 5.

When we come to look into *ch.* 4 we discover that, like other parts of the Historical Books, it is composite in structure. The main body of the narrative is enclosed in a framework which can be readily detected; and we could hardly find a clearer specimen of the method or scheme of the Redactor, who is responsible for this framework.

A. We will deal first with this element in *ch.* 4. As in the case of Othniel (3, 7–11), Ehud (3, 12–30), Gideon (6, 1–7. 8, 28), Jephthah (10, 6. 7. 10. 11, 33ᵇ. 12, 7), Samson (13, 5. 15, 20. 16, 31), the Redactor takes the story of Deborah and Barak and fits it into his regular scheme[1]. This scheme is based upon a theory of the period of the Judges which is announced in 2, 11–19. National apostasy and sin, such as always occurred after the death of the last Judge, is followed by a period of oppression[2]; Jehovah sells His unfaithful people into the hand of their enemies[3]; they cry unto Jehovah, and He raises up a deliverer, a judge[4], who becomes the divine instrument in the subjugation[5] of the oppressors. After the victory the land has rest for forty years[6]. Such being

---

[1] Driver, *Introduction*, 1892, pp. 154, 155. Budde, *Richter und Samuel*, 1890, p. 93.

[2] לחץ 2, 18. 6, 9. 10, 12; cf. 1, 34.

[3] A characteristic figure of the compiler, cf. 2, 14–3, 8. 4, 2. 10, 7; similarly 1 Sa. 12, 9. Ezra 30, 12. Cf. ψ. 44, 13. Probably derived from Dt. 32, 30.

[4] הושיע, שפט 2, 16. 18. 3, 9 f. 15. 4, 4. 10, 1 ff. 13. 12, 8 ff. 13 f. 15, 20. 16, 31; cf. 2, 19. 6, 9. 9, 22. 10, 12.

[5] כנע 3, 30. 4, 23. 8, 28. 11, 33. These last two expressions form such integral parts of the narratives to which they are attached, that it has been thought that they may be due to the *pre*-Deuteronomic compiler. Driver, *ib.*, p. 157.

[6] שקט 3, 11. 30 ('twenty'). 5, 31. 8, 28. Cf. Jos. 11, 23. 14, 15 Δ. Wellhausen, *Composition*, p. 218.

the Redactor's scheme, the parts due to his hand in our two chapters are clearly 4, 1-3. 23. 24. 5, 31[b]. This time the enemy is Jabin, king of Canaan; Hazor is the seat of his kingdom, and Sisera of Harosheth the general of his army; and for twenty years he had mightily afflicted Israel. Against this Canaanite oppressor God raises up a judge in the person of the prophetess Deborah, who, with Barak, defeats the enemy by God's help, and brings about a lasting peace for forty years.

This is the Redactor's account of what occurred. Two things strike us at once as presenting difficulties which cast doubt upon the accuracy of his narrative. (1) The title 'king of Canaan' (4, 2. 23. 24 *bis*); as though 'Canaan' were an organized kingdom united under a single head, while in fact it was a general name for a number of independent tribes, each with a chief of its own, no doubt of the same race, but certainly not bound together under a federal government (cf. Josh. 5, 1. 9, 1. 11, 1. 2. 12, 19-24). Moreover, the title contradicts the express statement of the Song (5, 19), 'then fought the *kings* of Canaan.' (2) The remark that Sisera, Jabin's general, dwelt at Harosheth, in a town of his own, far away from his chief, apparently holding an independent position, and directing the movements of the army entirely on his own responsibility. If, as seems most probable, Harosheth is to be identified with the modern el-Harithîje on the right bank of the lower Kishon, N. W. of Megiddo[1], then Sisera's town will

---

[1] Baedeker, *Palest. und Syrien*, ed. 1891, p. 241; Bertheau, *Richter u. Ruth*, 2nd ed., 1883, p. 84, though he wrongly places the village on the left bank of the river; Budde, p. 68. Kiepert, in his map of Palestine (1891), places both Harosheth and Hazor in a different locality. He identifies Harosheth with Haris, about 18 miles north of the modern Hazûr (i. e. Hazor, acc. to Kiepert), which lies a little to N. W. of Sea of Galilee. In either case the argument above will hold good. It is more probable, however, that Hazor was near the lake of Hûle, S.W. of the modern Dèschûn, and S. of Kedesh. So Pal. Expl. Fund's map, 1890, and Baed. Hazor is mentioned as Hazar in the list of the places in Palestine conquered by Thothmes III; on the Tel el-Amarna tablets it is called Khazura. *Records of the Past*, New Series, pp. 45 and 89.

have been at least forty miles south of Hazor. Is it likely
that the general and the army would have been stationed
so far away from the centre of the kingdom? Such a state
of things would be quite contrary to what we otherwise know
of the political conditions of the time. We notice, too, that
the 'nine hundred chariots of iron' belonging to Jabin in
v. 3 belong to Sisera in *v.* 13. In fact, the suspicion arises
that Sisera and Jabin are separated by more than a geographical distance from each other. Jabin apparently has nothing
to do with his general, and takes no part in the battle : he
is a motionless figure in the background. His name occurs
again in *v.* 7, 'captain of Jabin's army,' and in *v.* 17, 'for
there was peace between Jabin the king of Hazor and the
house of Heber the Kenite.' It has been thought, not without reason, that these words are merely glosses inserted by
the Redactor to make the narrative in *vv.* 4–22 fit into his
frame [1]. The narrative itself, when these words are struck out,
leaves the distinct impression that Sisera is an independent
chief, with an army of his own. He is the sole leader of
the campaign ; to kill him is to win the chief glory of the
battle (*v.* 9) ; he is in fact a Canaanite king. The mention
of Jabin in this chapter presents another difficulty. Hazor,
his town, was a few miles south of Kedesh ; accordingly the
negotiations that are said to have passed between Deborah
and Barak must have crossed his territory, and Barak's army
of 10,000 men must have been allowed to muster unmolested,
almost under the shadow of the enemy's walls. Moreover,
Heber's tent, which is said to have been by Kedesh, cannot
therefore have been far from Hazor; so that when Sisera
fled after the battle to Jael's tent he must have crossed the
kingdom of Jabin on his way. It is hardly credible that
he would have sought shelter with a stranger, when his own
people and his own patron were so close at hand. For these
reasons, then, we conclude that Jabin does not really belong

---

[1] So Bertheau, p. 83.

to the main narrative of *ch.* 4, and that he has been brought
into connexion with the Deborah-story through some accident
or misunderstanding. Jabin, king of Hazor, is found again
in Josh. 11 (JE) ; and there can be no doubt that it is he
who has been introduced into the narrative here. But as
a full discussion of this question concerns more than the
Redactor's portions of *ch.* 4, it must be reserved until we have
treated *vv.* 4–22. But what does concern us here is this :
did the Redactor himself connect Jabin with this history,
or did he find the connexion already made before he added
his framework ? It is clear that the Redactor must have
found the narrative *vv.* 4–22 already in existence, because he
provides it with an introduction and conclusion. But, as was
suggested above, he may have manipulated the text to make
it agree with his view, and the fact that Jabin agrees so
badly with the context, as has been shewn, supports this
opinion. On the other hand it is, perhaps, worth noticing
that in *v.* 7 the name Jabin occurs alone, and in *v.* 17 we
find ' Jabin king of Hazor,' and this is the title given in
Josh. 11; the Redactor's expression is 'king of Canaan.' If the
Redactor is solely responsible for Jabin, we of course conclude
that the name may be withdrawn from *ch.* 4 without any loss
to the narrative beyond the removal of a disturbing element.
Does the narrative (4–22), then, become more consistent
and intelligible when Jabin is struck out ? It is very doubtful whether it does ; for, as will be shewn later, we are almost
driven to the conclusion that more of Jabin than his mere
name exists in *ch.* 4, that, in fact, tradition wove together
two distinct histories of Jabin and Sisera. As there was
only room for one king, and Jabin came first in order of time,
Sisera had to be degraded into the ' captain of his host.'
So, on the whole, we believe that the Redactor found the
connexion between the two already made when he incor-
porated the tradition into his work [1].

---

[1] Kuenen, *Die historischen Bücher d. A. T.* (Germ. transl., 1890), p. 14, says
that there is no reason for supposing that *vv.* 7 and 17 have been interpolated.

There are traces of the Redactor's hand in three other
parts of *ch.* 4, in *v.* 4[b], in *v.* 9 a β, and in *v.* 14[a]. The
phrasing of 4[b], 'she judged (ptcp.) Israel at that time,'
suggests the point of view announced in 2, 16 and 3, 10—
both passages belonging to the compiler. The older narratives distinctly imply that the Judges were 'merely local
heroes;' their authority hardly extended beyond their own
people and the tribes immediately around them. But the
later historian generalizes their position, and gives them a
jurisdiction extending over all Israel (e. g. 3, 10. 9, 22. 10, 2.
12, 8-9. 16, 31 etc.)[1]. *Ver.* 4[b] is expressed in accordance with
this view. That it is a generalization appears also from the
fact that Deborah is said to have 'judged Israel' during
the period of the oppression; and that her influence and
authority had been long established before the overthrow of
the Canaanites. In the case of the other Judges, their rule
always begins after they have vindicated their right to be
leaders by some signal victory over the enemy.

In *v.* 9 a β we meet with the characteristic expression,
'Jehovah will *sell* . . into the hand [of a woman].' As has
been already remarked, this is a favourite figure of the compiler. Finally, in *v.* 14, 'Jehovah hath given [Sisera] in thy
hand,' is probably another phrase of the same writer (cf. 3,
28. Jos. 8, 18. 10, 8 Δ).

B. So much for the Redactor. He gives us not so much
history, as what Prof. A. B. Davidson calls 'the religious
philosophy of history[2].' But fortunately he incorporates
earlier traditions and documents which enable us to go behind
his statements, and reach firmer historical foot-hold. When
his contributions to the story have been extracted, there
remains the bulk of the narrative, contained in *vv.* 4-22.

---

[1] Driver, *Introd.*, p. 157. Yet this generalization dates from early times,
and probably was 'a trait due to the first compiler;' it 'is so associated with
the individual narratives that it must have formed a feature in them before
they came into the hands of the Deuteronomic compiler.'
[2] *Expositor*, Jan. 1887, p. 48.

We have to examine the tradition it embodies and its value
as a historical source. Accordingly, we will first give an
account of its contents, and then point out the features in
which it agrees, and next those in which it disagrees, with
ch. 5, and finally estimate its character and worth. There
will be some uncertain and difficult ground to traverse before
we reach the firm rock.

1. Contents. Deborah, a prophetess, the wife of Lappidoth,
dwelling under a well-known palm tree in the south of
Ephraim, between Ramah and Bethel, summons the warrior
Barak of Kedesh-naphtali in the far north, to help her to
form a combination to resist the Canaanite enemy. He is to
march towards Tabor with 10,000 men of Naphtali and
Zebulun, and she will attract Sisera and his army to the
torrent Kishon. Barak refuses to undertake the campaign
unless the prophetess go with him. She consents, but, as
a punishment for his hesitation, promises the chief glory of
the war, the slaying of Sisera, not to him but to a woman.
So Deborah sets out with Barak for Kedesh in the north,
where the two clans are mustered, 10,000 strong, and the
march to Tabor begins. Sisera is informed of the movement;
he gathers his forces, and proceeds from Harosheth along the
Kishon valley. The critical moment has come. The two
armies engage somewhere in the alluvial tract which runs
N.E. from the plain of Esdraelon to the foot of Tabor[1].
Jehovah discomfits Sisera, and all his chariots, and all his
host, and Sisera himself is forced to fly. The Canaanites
retreat to Harosheth whither Barak pursues them, while Sisera
flies in a north-easterly direction as far as Kedesh. Jael,
the wife of the Kenite Heber, gives him shelter and refresh-
ment, and then treacherously murders him as he lies asleep
by driving a tent-peg into his temples. Barak comes up,
and finds his enemy slain.

[1] Probably the broad valley or plain watered by the W. el-Muwēli, an
offshoot from the Kishon.

2. These are the contents of the narrative. How do they appear when compared with our standard authority, *ch.* 5? In the main features the prose account is in agreement with the Song. The chief actors are the same, Deborah, Barak, Sisera, and Jael. The formidable Canaanites are overthrown in a signal victory by the help of Jehovah, and Sisera himself is murdered by Jael, after she had given him food and shelter in her tent. Zebulun and Naphtali are mentioned as taking part in the battle, and the torrent Kishon is the one geographical term common to both versions. Thus we have in *ch.* 4 all the essentials of the drama, the *dramatis personae*, the main action or motive, the final *dénouement*, and a hint as to the scene. In these essential points *ch.* 4 agrees with *ch.* 5, and that means, according to the canon we have laid down, that *ch.* 4 has preserved a true tradition of the main facts of the story. These points, then, will form the element of accurate history in *ch.* 4.

3. But in many respects the two accounts exhibit striking differences. Of course allowance must be made for the fact that one is in prose and the other in poetry; but the Song is so full of living impressions of persons and places, and is so near to the events themselves, that it may be freely used for comparative and constructive purposes. For the sake of clearness we may gather these differences into three groups, according as they are concerned with the persons engaged in the battle, the circumstances and geography of the campaign, and the Jael-episode.

a. The persons engaged in the battle : Deborah. According to *ch.* 4, as we have seen, she comes from the hill-country of Ephraim, apparently from the territory of Benjamin. In *ch.* 5 it is at any rate implied (*v.* 15) that she belongs to the tribe of Issachar[1]. There is nothing in the Song to suggest that she

---

[1] Reuss, however, *Gesch. d. heil. Schr. d. A. T.*, 2nd ed., 1890, p. 126, says that the text is too uncertain here to build this conclusion upon it. But see Wellhausen, *Composition*, p. 221; Stade, *Geschichte*, i. p. 178; Budde, p. 104; Driver, *Introd.*, p. 162.

had been a Judge for some time before the victory; it is in fact stated, as we should expect, that she arose to meet the emergency and put an end to the disorders (*v.* 7). Barak, too, is also associated with the tribe of Issachar (*v.* 15), while in *ch.* 4 he comes from Kedesh in Naphtali, and evidently belongs to that tribe (4, 6). There is no trace in the Song of Barak's hesitation and consequent punishment—the forfeiture of the chief glory of the battle. If we adopt the reading 'lead captive thy captors' (Luther, Wellh., Stade, Budde, Kittel, etc.) in *v.* 12, Barak had suffered so much at the enemy's hands that he would not have needed much stirring up. The divergences in the two accounts extend further. In *ch.* 4 it said that only Naphtali and Zebulun engaged in the war, and that the army of 10,000 was gathered entirely from their two tribes. In the Song it is very different. Six tribes, both from the north and from the south, Ephraim, Benjamin, Machir (i. e. West Manasseh), Zebulun, Issachar, Naphtali, respond to the summons of Deborah and Barak. Everything is on a more imposing scale; the campaign is an affair of national concern; the call to arms goes round to all the organized tribes, and bitter, mocking irony is hurled at those who refused to respond (5, 15[b]-17); for Jehovah Himself, the national God, descends to take part in the battle (*v.* 23). And not only Deborah and Barak but the chiefs of the various tribes take their places as leaders (*rv.* 2. 9. 12. 15). As the Israelite forces in *ch.* 5 are of greater magnitude, so the enemy is more formidable. Sisera does not appear alone, as in *ch.* 4, but he is the head of a confederation of Canaanite kings (*v.* 19).

b. There are considerable differences, too, in the circumstances and geography connected with the war. As Wellhausen points out[1], in *ch.* 5 the picture is not so much of a land subdued by the enemy and 'mightily oppressed' (4, 2. 3), as of a land rendered insecure and harassed by constant inroads. The area of the battle is not the same in the two chapters.

[1] *Composition,* p. 221.

According to *ch.* 4 the army is mustered in the far north, in Kedesh, and then marches to Tabor (*v.* 9), and takes up a strong position commanding the plain below. The offensive movement begins with a descent from the mountain, and the actual engagement takes place on the broad levels at the foot [1]. In *ch.* 5 there is no mention either of Kedesh or of Tabor; the battle is fought along the right bank of the Kishon (*vv.* 19. 21) [2], whose torrent, swollen by a heavy storm (not mentioned in the prose narrative), materially furthers the Israelite victory (*v.* 21); in *ch.* 4 the battle-field is on the left side of the Kishon. We gather that it was Issachar who had been the principal sufferer at the hands of king Sisera; the two chief leaders belong to this tribe, and the battle takes place entirely within its territory. Naphtali and Zebulun are the generous allies who boldly risked themselves for the deliverance of their brother-tribe. Wellhausen seems to exaggerate when he says [3] that in *ch.* 4 the victory is won entirely by Divine intervention, while in *ch.* 5 all is due to human exertions. In both accounts all the available forces are collected and manœuvred, and in both Jehovah lends His divine assistance (4, 9. 14. 15. 5, 4. 13. 23. Note esp. Jehovah's 'going down' to the battle, 4, 14 and 5, 13).

c. The last important difference between the two versions lies in the accounts given of the murder of Sisera by Jael. In *ch.* 4 she takes a tent-pin in one hand and a hammer in the other, and treacherously murders him while he is asleep, by driving the tent-pin through his temples. In *ch.* 5, on the other hand, while he is *standing* and drinking eagerly out of the deep bowl [4], she comes behind and deals him a

---

[1] In 4, 7. 13 נחל קישון will mean the Kishon torrent-*valley*, while in 5, 19 the same words denote the *torrent* itself.

[2] In *ch.* 4, the verb describing the army on march is עלה (*vv.* 10. 12), Barak's object being to entrench himself firmly in a mountain position. In *ch.* 5 the verb is ירד (*vv.* 11. 13, cf. 15); the combined forces pour down the Kishon valley.

[3] *Prolegomena,* p. 249.

[4] ספל אדירים 'a lordly bowl,' the great bowl only used on special occasions

terrific blow with a hammer (*v.* 26). This puts a different complexion upon what otherwise appears to be an act of cruel treachery; in reality it was a bold stratagem swiftly planned and daringly carried out. As such it wins the praise accorded in *vv.* 24–27.

4. According to the principle laid down, those features which *ch.* 4 has in common with *ch.* 5 and in which it differs from the earlier authority will be of inferior historical value. The *external* evidence which has just been adduced from the Song substantiates this opinion ; the *internal* evidence of the narrative itself points in the same direction. *a.* It has been already noticed (§ A) that the generalization of the position and jurisdiction of Deborah betrays the influence of a later age, and is at variance with the impression we gain from the rest of the story. There is a further point, about her relations with Barak, which must be mentioned here. The prophetess is made to dwell in the south, between Ramah and Beth-el. This necessitates distant negotiations with Barak in the far north, so that Deborah's messengers must have crossed right through the very heart of the enemy's territory ; to get to Kedesh they would have to pass Hazor, the town of Jabin, according to the narrative as it now stands. The interval between the two leaders strikes us as strange. The Ephraimite Deborah has no obvious connexion with an affair which concerned only the tribes of Naphtali and Zebulun. In other cases where a Judge is raised up to deliver his people he is a member of the suffering tribe, and dwells in the immediate vicinity of the enemy's aggressions. But Deborah lives in the south, far from the centre of the troubles ; she brings no reinforcements of her own to join the northern army; she is simply the counsellor of the chieftain of another tribe. How came she to be thus separated from Barak and the seat of the war? There is nothing in *ch.* 5 to suggest a connexion

and for distinguished guests. The word only occurs again in 6, 38. In 4, 19 the word is נאד, i.e. a skin-'bottle.'

between her and Ephraim. The most probable explanation
of the difficulty is to suppose that tradition has confused her
with the earlier Deborah, Rebekah's nurse, whose grave was
'below Beth-el under the terebinth of Bachuth' (Gen. 35, 8) [1].
In this way the prophetess became connected with the south,
and had to carry on communication with Barak at a distance.
Accordingly *vv.* 5. 6*a.* 9 *end* will be based upon this confusion [2].

b. There is another doubtful feature in our narrative, which
admits, though with less probability, of a similar explanation
—the position of Kedesh. The town mentioned in *vv.* 6. 9.
10. 11 is Kedesh in Naphtali, also called Kedesh in Galilee
(Josh. 20, 7. 21, 32. 1 Chr. 6, 76), situated near the Lake
of Ḥûle (? Merom), and one of the most important towns in
the north. After the battle Barak pursues the Canaanites in
a north-westerly direction as far as Harosheth, while Sisera
flies towards the north-east, to Kedesh, nearly 40 miles from
the battle-field. And yet Barak comes up to Heber's tent (by
Kedesh) only a short while after Sisera, who had fled there
direct. Here is a manifest inconsistency. Barak follows the
retreat of the Canaanites in one direction, and then pursues
Sisera for some forty miles in exactly the opposite direction,
yet he is only a few steps behind him !

Again we may suppose that there has been some confusion.
Kedesh in Naphtali, it has been suggested [3], was confused
with Kedesh in Issachar, situated between Taanach and

---

[1] So Wellh., Stade, Budde. Cf. 1 Sa. 10, 3 אלון הבור near Bethel;
Berth. suggests that 'א רבורה should be read. But Reuss (*Gesch. d. heil.
Schr. d. A. T.*, p. 126) objects that Deborah here is said to have dwelt
under a well-known palm-tree (המר), while the other Deborah was buried
under a *terebinth* (אלון). The objection seems rather trifling, and Wellh.
(*Proleg.*, p. 246 *n.*) points out that the two words might mean the same thing—
e. g. Elim (אלים) is the name for an oasis of seventy palm-trees, and Elath
(אילת) by the Red Sea has perhaps the same meaning. At any rate tradition
might easily have confused the two words. See also Robertson Smith, *Rel.
of Semites*, p. 179 *n.*

[2] Budde, p. 70 *n.*, is disposed to strike out the whole of *v.* 9, and *v.* 8 as
well.

[3] Reuss, *ib.*, p. 126; Wellh., *Comp.*, p. 221.

Mcgiddo in the Kishon-valley [1]. This is a convenient solution
of the difficulty. If it be right, everything will fall into its
proper place: the area of the campaign will be the plains
lying about the Kishon; Barak of Kedesh becomes a member
of the tribe of Issachar, as is implied in *ch. 5.* Moreover, the
tent of Heber, pitched 'as far as the terebinth in Zaannim [2]
which is by Kedesh' (4, 11), will have lain on the route of the
retreat; Barak as he pursues [3] the Canaanites turns aside and
finds his enemy lying slain. Thus the difficulty connected
with the flight of Sisera disappears, and the account is brought
into agreement with *ch. 5.* But the question remains, how
did Kedesh get into the narrative? There is no Kedesh in
the Song from which the confusion could have arisen. This
is one of the points in which the prose account goes beyond
the original authority, and we prefer to explain the occurrence
in a different way, viz. that Kedesh is part of an independent
tradition, which originally belonged to quite a different event.
And it will be found that this is the most probable explanation
to be given of the remaining parts of *ch. 4* which contain
matter which seems suspicious when contrasted with *ch. 5.*

c. Stade [4] explains the statement that Barak had an army of
only 10,000 men drawn from only two tribes, Naphtali and
Zebulun, as modified in the interests of religious edification.
The victory was gained solely by the might of Jahweh; man
had little or nothing to do with it. So too, Barak was
punished for his hesitation and want of faith by having to
yield the chief glory of the battle to a woman in order to
point a religious moral. This may be true of *vv.* 8 and 9, but
hardly of *vv.* 6 and 10. What is said here of Naphtali and

[1] 1 Chr. 6, 57. Josh. 12, 22 (as context shews).
[2] Ewald, *History*, ii. p. 377 *n.*, writes it 'the terebinth of Bezaannim,' i.e.
'of the marsh-dwellers' (נצב = marsh). So Wellh. 'Elon Besaanim.' The name
would be as suitable for the neighbourhood of the Kishon-torrent as for the
marshy land about the Lake of Ḥûle.
[3] Point רדף (ptcp.), *v.* 16. LXX διώκων. Budde, p. 68.
[4] *Geschichte*, i. p. 178 *n.*

Zebulun most probably belongs to the same tradition as Kedesh; the position of the town suggests the connexion. So far, then, we have discovered the traces of some story concerned with the early history of these two tribes and the muster of the clan-warriors in Kedesh against some common foe in the north country.

d. Another element in the same tradition is most probably to be found in the prose version of the Jael-episode. It is true that many scholars prefer to explain the peculiarities of this account by supposing that they are due to a misunderstanding of the parallelism in *v.* 26 of the Song. According to the laws of Hebrew poetry, 'she put her hand to the peg' or pin, i.e. the handle of the hammer, might very well mean the same thing as 'and her right hand to the workmen's mallet.' The word 'peg' 'suggested a tent-peg, and so the later prose story took it, and thereby misunderstood the whole thing.' So writes Prof. Robertson Smith[1]. But Kuenen and Budde are probably right in refusing to admit that the divergence arose from a misunderstanding of the words 'peg' and 'hammer[2].' The whole account of the Jael-episode in *ch.* 4 must be ascribed to a secondary tradition, according to which Jael murders Sisera in his sleep.

Thus the result of our comparison of the two accounts will be this: they are agreed as to the main facts; but *ch.* 4 exhibits considerable divergences from *ch.* 5, the chief authority for the history, and these divergences consequently possess inferior historical value, internal evidence being also against them; at the same time some of these divergences contain matter

---

[1] *The Old Testament in the Jewish Church*, 2nd ed., p. 132. Wellh., *Comp.*, p. 222, was the first to suggest that יתד and הלמות mean the same thing, likewise ירה (not שמאלה) and ימינה. Cf. Zech. 9, 9 with Mat. 21, 2. 7. So Stade, *Geschichte*, i. p. 178 *n.*

[2] A. Müller in *Königsberger Studien*, i. 1887, p. 20, says that neither in Hebrew nor in Arabic can יתד mean anything but 'a peg,' i.e. a tent-peg. وَتِد always = a wooden pin, peg, or stake, fixed in the ground or in a wall; Lane, s. v. Müller characterizes both יתד and צמלים הלמות as doubtful.

which goes beyond the history that lies in the background of
the Song, and seems to belong to a different tradition. It
has been noticed that neither Jabin, Kedesh, nor Tabor are
found in *ch.* 5, and the mention of all three introduces serious
disturbance into the narrative. There is one other name
found only in *ch.* 4, that of Lappidoth, Deborah's husband
(*v.* 4). Now we have seen (*a*, above) that Deborah is brought
into relation with Ramah and Bethel through a confusion
based on Gen. 35, 8. Originally, then, according to *ch.* 4,
she dwelt at Kedesh, the city of Barak, and set out with him
from their common dwelling-place. This agrees with the
impression that we gain from 5, 15 that Deborah and Barak
were themselves of the same tribe, though here it is Issachar.
Both in the song and in the narrative (5, 12–15. 4, 6 etc.)
they appear as though they were intimately connected with
one another. Now it is remarkable that both Barak ('lightning')
and Lappidoth ('flames,' Ex. 20, 18) mean very nearly the same
thing; it is but a step further to conclude that they are the
same person [1]. The words 'the wife of Lappidoth' occur in a
verse which we have seen reason to believe has been influenced
by the Redactor's point of view. So it is at least *possible*
that these words date from the same period, and that a later
age had preserved Barak's second name, and made him the
husband, though in the earlier tradition he is only the fellow-
tribesman, of Deborah.

We are now in a position to form some idea of the way
in which the narrative in *ch.* 4 assumed its present form.
Woven together, and largely modified so as to form a con-
secutive narrative, are two independent traditions, the one
relating to Jabin, the other to Sisera.

To the Jabin-tradition will belong such facts as cannot
naturally be brought into agreement with the history contained in the Song. This tradition, in fact, related the early

---

[1] The suggestion was first made by Hilliger, *Das Deborah-lied*, Giessen,
1867. He is followed by Well., *Comp.*, p. 223, and Budde, p. 69.

fortunes of *Naphtali* and *Zebulun* in the early days when
their newly-won possessions were still insecure [1]. The neighbouring Canaanites under Jabin, king of Hazor, combined to
resist the intruders. The two clans assembled all their available warriors, and made Kedesh their head-quarters. Marching out from here they encountered Jabin, and won a decisive
victory. This ancient tradition forms the basis of the later
account of the battle of Merom given in Josh. 11, 1-9 (JE),
which contains many traces of the Deuteronomic redaction; and,
as Budde suggests it is probable that the compiler of Joshua
chose the tradition of an ancient battle in the far north to
complete his number of three representative victories occurring
in upper, middle (at Ai, Josh. 8), and lower Palestine (at
Gibeon, Josh. 10). In some way or other Barak (? and
Deborah) became connected with the Jabin-tradition, just as
Joshua is made the leader in the other form of the story
(Josh. 11).

The remaining part of our narrative (of course excepting
the parts due to the Redactor) is derived from a Sisera-
tradition, which forms a secondary narrative of the events
which were the occasion of the Song. This tradition is concerned with the fortunes of the tribe of *Issachar*. The
Canaanites in the Kishon valley combined under Sisera, king
of Harosheth, to harass the Israelite settlers; until their
intermittent attacks culminated in a pitched battle fought
out at the foot of Mount Tabor, all within the territory of
Issachar. Deborah and Barak led the Israelite army, and,
with the help of Jehovah, inflicted a severe defeat upon the
enemy. The Canaanites were forced by Barak to retreat
upon Harosheth, and Sisera himself had to fly for his life.
He found shelter and food in the tent of the Kenite Jael, who
murdered him as he lay asleep, weary after the fight [2].

---

[1] The fact that this tradition speaks of only *two* tribes being engaged is
an evidence of its antiquity (Budde, p. 69), and connects it with the fragments in
1, 1-2, 5, which narrate the efforts of the separate tribes to win their territories.
[2] The contents of the two traditions as given here correspond generally with

How the two traditions came to be united is difficult to say. Perhaps the connexion was suggested by the fact that both were concerned with the fighting that took place in Upper Palestine when the northern tribes were engaged in securing their territories, and by the fact that Canaanites in both cases were the enemy. Budde thinks that the person of Barak formed the link between the two[1]. At any rate the historian combined the traditions in such a way as to make them agree in the essential features, and sacrificed secondary details.

That the Song had an historical introduction attached to it in early times is rendered probable by analogy. Bertheau[2] points out that the not very common word וַיָּהָם, 'discomfited,' occurring only here in Judges, is found in the prose counterpart to the Song of Moses (Ex. 14, 24 J), and again just before the poetic fragment in Josh. 10, 12. 13 (v. 10 JE, only here in Josh.).

C. It remains to give an outline of the history contained in the Song, our standard authority for what actually took place.

After a long period of oppression and insecurity which had lasted since the days of Shamgar, Deborah, a woman of

the parts assigned by Bruston to what he calls the Second and the First Jehovist. Bruston, however, attaches the Jael-episode to the Second Jehovist (Jabin-tradition), and confines Deborah to the First Jehovist (Sisera-tradition). Barak occurs in both. The weak points in this arrangement are the occurrence of Naphtali and Zebulun in both documents, and the association of Jael with the Jabin-story. *Revue de Théologie et de Philosophie*, 1885, pp. 501 ff., Les deux Jéhovist s, vi.

[1] Cf. Jos., *Ant.*, v. 5. 4. 'Barak also fought with Jabin at Hazor ; and when he met him he slew him : and when the general was fallen, Barak overthrew the city to the foundation, and was the commander of the Israelites for forty years.'

[2] *Richter u. Ruth*, 2nd ed., 1883, p. 85. He supposes that the main part of ch. 4 was attached to the Song in the collection from which the latter was derived. The unhistorical character of much of the narrative would not necessarily be an objection to Bertheau's view, for the historian must have lived at least two or three centuries later, and so might easily have had his ideas confused. Kuenen, p. 15.

martial spirit and fearless determination, together with Barak,
who probably himself had once been taken prisoner by the
enemy, resolve to free their people from the Canaanite
tyranny. Issachar, their tribe, had been the principal sufferer,
but could not cope with the formidable enemy unaided.
Accordingly the summons is sent round to all the tribes[1],
claiming their assistance for what was declared to be the
cause of Jehovah, the God of their fathers. For the first
time in its history Israel acts in a national capacity; it was
the genius and courage of Deborah that instigated this united
action. The tribes of Ephraim, Benjamin, West Manasseh,
Zebulun, and Naphtali, with their chiefs, rally round the
tribe of Issachar; Reuben, Gilead, Dan, and Asher refuse to
rouse themselves. To meet this warlike confederation the
kings of Canaan, under the leadership of Sisera, march to the
attack, and the battle takes place in the neighbourhood of
Taanach and Megiddo, along the right bank of the Kishon.
A tremendous storm comes on, and the swollen torrent works
havoc among the Canaanite forces, so that it seemed as if
the very powers of nature were fighting on the side of Israel.
A woman had successfully initiated the war, and a woman
brings it to a triumphant conclusion. Jael, by a bold stratagem,
slays king Sisera as he stands drinking in her tent.

But the Hebrew patriot could not tell of such deeds in
bare prose. The recollection of that eventful day stirred him
to praise Jehovah and recount the victory in passionate song.
Thus we have preserved to us not only the finest ode in
Hebrew literature, but also the most venerable authority for
a page in the history of ancient Israel.

---

[1] Simeon and Levi, of course, excepted. But it is noticeable that Judah is
not mentioned. It had not yet realized its corporate existence, and had not
entered into any close connexion with the other tribes.

PART II.

THE TEXT AND VERSIONS.

CHAPTER IV.

THERE is not much difficulty about the text of *ch.* 4. Only the most important points will be noticed here.

Verse 1. ‏וג׳ ‏ויספו‎] Formula, characteristic of the Red., as in 2, 11. 3, 7. 12. 10, 6. 13, 1.

‏ואהור מת‎] Circumstantial clause. Driver, *Tenses*, ed. 3, § 159. ‏מת‎ is pf. not ptcp.; cf. 8, 11ᵇ. Ruth 1, 21. etc.

4. ‏אשה נביאה‎] Cf. for similar apposition 6, 8 ‏איש נביא‎. Ex. 2, 13 ‏אנשים עברים‎. 1 K. 21, 10. 2 K. 2, 16. Jer. 43, 9. Deborah acts as a prophetess when she declares the will of Jehovah in regard to the war (*v.* 6), and when she determines the day for the battle (*v.* 14). The other prophetesses in the O.T. are Miriam (Ex. 15, 20), Hulda (2 K. 22, 14), and Noadiah (Neh. 6, 14).

5. ‏תחת תמר דבורה‎] Deborah is here represented as declaring the sacred oracle under a palm-tree near Bethel, which also marked the grave of Rachel's nurse, according to tradition —see Rob. Smith, *Rel. of Semites*, p. 179. For illustrations of trees being connected with Divine oracles cf. 9, 37 ‏אלון‎ ‏מעוננים‎ with Gen. 12, 6 ‏מורה א׳‎; Dt. 11, 30, and esp. 2 S. 5, 24. But we have seen reason to doubt the genuineness of this association of Deborah with the sacred tree. Budde (p. 70 *n.*) treats the words as a gloss on ‏יושבת‎, the meaning of which is consequently changed from 'dwelling' to 'sitting' (cf. 6, 11); but they rather seem to be due to the original confusion with Gen. 35. 8, which connected Deborah with Ramah and Bethel. The Targ. embroiders the text with an account of Deborah's 'palm-trees in Jericho, gardens in Ramah, olive trees yielding oil in the valley, irrigation wells (‏בית שקיא‎) in Bethel,' etc. The difference between the expressions in 4ᵇ and 5ᵇ is noticeable. The former betrays the influence of the compiler.

6. 7. ‏משך‎] is used in three ways: *a.* Intrans.=*draw out, deploy*, e.g. *v.* 6. 20, 37 ‏וימשך הארב‎, Ex. 12, 21, cf. Job 21, 33.

b. Intrans., with ב of instrument = *draw, prolong, move along,*
with, e.g. 5, 14. Dt. 21, 3. Josh. 6, 5 בקרן היובל, 1 K. 22, 34.
c. Trans., with accus. = *draw out, lead along, extend,* e.g. v. 7.
Gen. 37, 28. Jer. 38, 13. ψ. 10, 9. Hos. 11, 4 (חסד). etc.

6. קדש] (Naphtali). Here and in *vv.* 9. 10. 11 Pesh. has
ܩܕ݂ܫ, as in Josh. 12, 22. 1 Chr. 6, 76. 72 (Kedesh in Issachar);
but in Josh. 19, 37. 21, 32 ܩܕ݂ܫ, and in 15, 23 for K. in
Judah. The Targ. always gives קדש in these places. For
Kadesh (Barnea) in S. of Pal., the Pesh. writes ܩܕ݂ܫ (e.g. Gen.
14, 7. 16, 14. 20, 1 etc.) or ܩܕ݂ܫ ܒܪܢܥ (Num. 32, 8. 34, 4.
Dt. 1, 2. 19 etc.), except in Num. 33, 36. 37. ψ. 29, 8 (ܩܕ݂ܫ).
The Targg. *always* have רקם or רקם גיאה (גיאה spelt in different
ways) for this Kadesh. Arab. الرقيم. There was evidently a tradition of another name for Kadesh Barnea, consistently preserved in the Targg., and partially in the Pesh., the latter
sometimes (through confusion) giving the name to the different
towns called Kedesh in the north.

ותשלח and מקדש נ׳ must be due to the historian who
placed Deborah in the S., and so made it necessary for her to
summon Barak from Kedesh.

7. את סיסרא שר צבא יבין] These words mark the con-
fluence of the two traditions of Jabin and Sisera which must
have been united before the time of the Red. (see p. 5), who
adopted the expression into his framework, *v.* 2.

8. LXX. adds ὅτι οὐκ οἶδα τὴν ἡμέραν ἐν ᾗ εὐοδοῖ τὸν ἄγγελον
Κύριος μετ᾽ ἐμοῦ B. so Luc. κ̄ς̄ τὸν ἄγγελον A. Syr.-Hex.
The sentence is not found in the other Verss.; it is merely a
gloss. On this verse see above, p. 13.

9. אפם כי] = *howbeit,* qualifying the preceding statement;
cf. Num. 13, 28. Dt. 15, 4. Am. 9, 8. 1 S. 1, 5 (corrected).
אפם is primarily a noun = *ceasing,* then it = *non-existence,* and
so comes to be used as a particle of negation, e.g. Is. 5, 8,
and, finally, as an adv. of limitation. The new *Hebr. Lex.,*
Clar. Pr. 1892, s.v. LXX. πλὴν γίνωσκε ὅτι.

ותקם ד׳ ותלך . . . קדשה] Another harmonizing addition,
to be grouped with 5ᵃ and 6ᵃ. LXX, Luc., ἐκ Κάδης. Perhaps
the LXX. took the view that the campaign begins in this verse,
and therefore chose to ignore the accus. ending (קדשה = *to*

Kedesh). In the next verse the same form is translated ἐκ Κάδης B. εἰς K'. A. Luc. Pesh. ܡܢ ܩܕܫ.

11ª. Both here and in 1, 16 (a most ancient document, probably of same age as J) the Kenites are brought into close relation with the father-in-law of Moses ; in fact it is implied here that Hobab was a Kenite. In the time of Moses the Kenites were settled about Sinai, and had attached themselves to the Midianites. So close was the alliance that the tribe of nomads was content to adopt the name of its more powerful patron, so that Moses' father-in-law, the priest of Kain or the Kenites, could be called 'the priest of Midian' (Ex. 2, 16), 'the Midianite' (Num. 10, 29 JE). How readily a nomad tribe could ally itself with a more powerful nation is shewn by the subsequent history of this clan, as far as it can be traced. Not only did their chief priest give his daughter to Moses for wife, but he willingly lent the Israelites all the assistance he could on the journey through the wilderness (Num. 10, 29 ff.), and this kindness was ever remembered with gratitude (1 S. 15, 6). In spite of the refusal of Hobab to cast in his lot with Israel (Num. 10, 30), it appears that some part of the Kenites allied themselves with Judah, and, in the early days of that tribe's settlement in W. Palestine, left their former habitation and found a home in the desert of Judah, south of Arad (Jud. 1, 16). In the same way the Kenites formed an alliance with the Amalekites : they are associated together in Balaam's prophecy (Num. 24, 21 f. JE), and in the time of Saul they were dwelling side by side in the south (1 S. 15, 5 ff.). They were on intimate terms with David ; he sends them presents from his spoil (1 S. 30, 29). Our verse tells how a certain family of the clan, that of Heber, branched off from the chief settlement and moved into the north, where it was destined to play an important part in this crisis of Israel's history.

The connexion of the Kenites with Moses through his father-in-law seems to have been dwelt upon with special satisfaction. It is twice emphatically mentioned in this book, Jud. 1, 16 and 4, 11. In the former place קיני (for קין) is called the father-in-law of Moses ; but the name merely denotes the representative or chief of the tribe. In our verse his name is חבב, which only occurs again in Num. 10, 29 'Hobab the son of Reuel the Midianite the father-in-law of Moses.' Which of the two are we to take as the father-in-law? If Reuel, then Hobab must be Moses' brother-in-law. But Reuel only occurs again in Ex. 2, 18, where its originality is open to question (Driver, *Introd.*, p. 21). Stade explains it as the name of a family or clan. At any rate the name Hobab seems the better attested. According to another tradition, that of E, Moses' relative was called Jethro, Ex. 3, 1. 4, 18. 18, 1 ff. Jud. 1, 16 LXX. B inserting 'Ιοθορ, but A. Luc. 'Ιωβαβ. See Stade, *Geschichte*, i. pp. 131 f.

אלון בצענים] Mentioned again in Josh. 19, 33 P (אלן בצעננים); in the territory of Naphtali. Here it is said to be 'by Kedesh.' It is not certain whether the ב is the prep. or part of the root. Tradition is in favour of the latter alternative, Josh. l.c. R.V.M. Targ. Jon. here connects with בִּצָּה *marsh*, מישר אגניא; so Talm. Jer., *Megila* i. אגניא, followed by Ewald, *History*, ii. p. 377 n. But בצה from √בצץ can hardly be connected with בצע. LXX. B and Θ also make the ב radical, ἕως δρυὸς πλεονεκτούντων (בצע). But Cod. A and Luc. confuse with שאננים, πρὸς δρῦν ἀναπαυομένων. Pesh. takes ב as prep. and transliterates the Hebr. Vulg., ad vallem quae vocatur Sennim. The omission of the rel. and of the art. with אלון favours the view that ב is radical; so rend. 'the terebinth of Bezaanim.'

15. ויהם] See p. 17.

לפי חרב] lit. *according to the mouth of the sword*, i. e. according to its capacity for devouring. This expression, generally with הכה, occurs regularly in the accounts of the exterminating wars against the Canaanites and Amalekites, e.g. Gen. 34, 26 J. Ex. 17, 13 E. Num. 21, 34 JE. Josh. 6, 21. 8, 24 JE. 10, 28 ff. 11, 11 ff. Δ (13 times). Jud. 1, 8. 25. 4, 15. 16. 18, 27. 1 S. 15, 8; and in those parts of the historical books which recall the old Canaanite wars, Jud. 20, 37. 48. 21, 10. 1 S. 22, 19. 2 S. 15, 14. 22, 19. 2 K. 10, 25 etc. Bertheau on 1, 8. He conjectures that the phrase must have stood in the older narratives which originally related these wars.

16. Point רֹדֵף. See p. 13 n.

עד חרשת] LXX. B ἕως Ἀρείσωθ. ἕως δρυμοῦ A. Luc., connecting with חרש = *a wood*, Is. 17, 9. 1 S. 23, 15 f. 19 etc.

לא נשאר עד אחד] Cf. Ex. 14, 28 ?J. 8, 27. 9, 7. 10, 19 J. Bruston (see p. 17 *n.*) makes the 'First Jehovist,' i.e. the Sisera-tradition, end here, and the Song immediately follow.

17ᵇ. Another connecting-link (cf. 7ᵃ *n.*) due to the writer who wove together the Jabin- and Sisera-traditions before the time of the Redactor.

18. סורה אדני סורה אלי] The accent on the ultima in these forms when א, ה, ע follow, to avoid the hiatus, cf. ψ. 82, 8. Jud. 5, 12. Is. 51, 9. So when יהוה for אדני follows, Num. 10, 36. Ges. § 72. i. 3.

שׂמיכה] ἅ. λ. Derivation and exact meaning uncertain. In some MSS. written סמיכה, and in *Ochla Wᵉochla* (ed. Frensd., no. 191) placed among the 18 words in O. T. written with שׂ for ס. See also Kimchi, *Rad. Lib.* s. v. Perhaps its meaning may be illustrated from the uses of the root ܣܡܟ in Syr. = to sustain, lean upon, incumbere, etc. Hence ܡܣܡܟܐ = a reclining, accubitus, a seat for reclining, 1 S. 20, 25 Pesh. = συμπόσιον, Mk. 6, 39 = κλισία, Lk. 9, 14. Hence שמיכה may be something connected with reclining, the rug or blanket used to make up a tent-bed.

The Verss. give various renderings : LXX. ἐπιβολαίῳ B. ἐν τῇ δέρρει αὐτῆς A. Luc. ἐν τῷ σάγῳ, Θ. ἐν κοιμήτρῳ Σ. ܟܘܡܣܐ Pesh. בגונכא (= καννάκη) Targ. In pelle sua,V. L.; pallio,Vulg.

19. Another contrast between this account and that in 5, 25-27—Sisera asks for drink and Jael brings it to him *after* he has lain down and been covered with the tent-rug.

20. עמד] for עמדי the nearest gender, cf. Is. 32, 11 חרדו שאננות. Am. 4, 1. Mic. 1, 13. For the form of sentence, והיה . . . ואמרת, expressing a wish, entreaty, or injunction, cf. 9, 33 ופשטת . . . והיה. 11, 31 ; with impf. in apod. 7, 4. 17. Driver, *Tenses*, § 121.

21. בלאט] The ptcp. of לוט with vowel-letter א, cf. קאם Hos. 10, 14. ראש 2 S. 12, 1. 4. Elsewhere the form is בּלּט 1 S. 18, 22. 24, 5. Ru. 3, 7. Ges. § 72. 1. 1 (N. B. The refs. to Ges. are to the 25th ed. by Kautzsch, 1889).

ותצנח] In the only two other places where it occurs this

rt. = *to alight, descend from,* Josh. 15, 18. Jud. 1, 14 מעל וַתִּצְנַח
הַחֲמוֹר. So here, 'it descended, went down, into the earth.'
LXX. διεξῆλθεν B. διήλασεν A. Luc. ܐܚܬ݁ܘ Pesh.; defixit,Vulg.
בארעא וּנעצת Targ. (cf. Targ. Gen. 28, 12=מצב, 30, 38).

נרדם [וְהוּא] perf.; a circumstantial clause. Tr. 'and he having fallen fast asleep,' cf. 3, 26. 16, 31. Driver, *Tenses,* § 160.

[וַיָּעַף] is introduced parenthetically : ' now (lit. and) he was
weary, and so he died.' This form comes from עיף, which only
occurs again in 1 S. 14, 28. 31. 2 S. 21, 15; cf. עיפה Jer. 4, 31.
Clause b. LXX. καὶ αὐτὸς ἐξεστῶς ἐσκοτώθη, καὶ ἀπέθανεν B.
καὶ αὐτὸς ἀπεσκάρισεν ἀνὰ μέσον τῶν γονάτων (ποδῶν Luc.) αὐτῆς,
καὶ ἐξέψυξεν, καὶ ἀπέθανεν A. Syr.-Hex. Some Codd. κεκαρωμένου
αὐτοῦ· ὁ δὲ ἐλειποθύμησεν. ἀποθανόντος δὲ αὐτοῦ (ἐφάνη Βαράκ) Σ.
The words ἀνὰ μέσον τῶν γον'. α'. in LXX. A are inserted from
5, 27. ܟܡ ܒ̈ܝ ܘܡܢܝ Pesh., so Targ., ' qui soporem
mortui consocians defuit, et mortuus est.'

22. [נָפַל] The ptcp. here of the immediate past, *fallen,*
not *falling.* Cf. 4, 22. Num. 24, 4. Dt. 21, 1. 1 S. 5, 4 ; cf. use
of מת = ' one lying dead,' ' a dead body.'

23. [אלהים] A mark of the Redactor's age and handiwork.
This name does not occur elsewhere in the narrative.

24. [הלוך וקשה] The inf. abs. is here carried on by the
ptcp. instead of another inf. abs.; cf. Gen. 26, 13 הלוך וְגָדֵל. 1 S.
14, 19. 2 S. 18, 25.

Chapter V.

Various analyses of the Song have been suggested, differing
considerably as to the grouping of details, but agreed in recog-
nizing a division into two main parts, viz. an introduction
leading up to the principal subject of the ode, and a description of the circumstances connected with the battle and
victory. It is generally agreed that the great break occurs
between vv. 11. 12. Ewald, indeed, was so impressed with the
difference between the first and second half of the Song that
he supposes two distinct poems to have been united, a song
of thanksgiving (2-11) and a song of victory (12-31). The

tone and character of the two parts differ fundamentally. In the former we find a summons to praise Jehovah, a thankful remembrance of His past dealings on behalf of the nation, a deep sense of His powerful share in the recent battle. But in the second part we pass from the divine to the human. The victory was due to the valour of the confederate army, the swollen Kishon, the heroism of Jael. (*Dichter d. Alten Bundes*, erster Theil, 2nd ed., 1865, p. 188.) But Ewald exaggerates the extent of the break after *v.* 11, and his view has not found favour with subsequent scholars. On the whole, the following analysis, in the main that of Bertheau, seems to commend itself.

PART I.

v. 2.	Prelude.			
vv. 3–5.	Retrospect of the Exodus . . .	Verse-members or *Stichoi*	9	⎫
vv. 6–8.	The recent period of oppression .	„	11	⎬ A.
vv. 9–11.	Summons to praise Jehovah . .	„	9	⎭

PART II.

v. 12.	Prelude to main subject.			
vv. 13–15ᶜ.	The mustering of the tribes . .	„	9	⎫
vv. 15ᵈ–18.	The reluctant and the ready . .	„	11	⎬ B.
vv. 19–21.	The battle	„	9	⎭
vv. 22–24.	After the battle	„	9	⎫
vv. 25–27.	The murder of Sisera	„	9	⎬ C.
vv. 28–30.	The anxiety and disappointment of his mother.	„	11	⎭
v. 31.	Conclusion.			

That the structure of the Song implies some strophical arrangement cannot be doubted. The one given above is perhaps as good as any other; at any rate it will serve as a starting-point. It will be noticed that there are three chief stanzas (A. B. C.), each containing three strophes. The three larger groups, moreover, display a symmetry of arrangement in the number of *stichoi* or verse-members belonging to each strophe, that is to say, in the text as it stands at present. But the text is by no means certain in several places, and the corrections which it will be found necessary to introduce have the effect of disturbing this apparent symmetry. For instance, in stanza C two *stichoi* must probably be struck out, so that the numbers will be 9. 8. 10. The originality of this stichical order is doubtful, and not to be entirely relied upon.

Another arrangement, turning on the number of *syllables*, not of verse-members, is that of Bickell (*Carmina V.T. metrice*, pp. 195 ff.). Applying his metrical principles, Bickell scans the Song by the 8.6 | 8.6 | 8.10 measure, to which he also adapts ψ. 86. Ex. 15, 1–18, Is. 12. This involves a treatment of the text and its pronunciation which seems arbitrary and hard to believe, though it often suggests valuable emendations.

One other scheme must be noticed, that of Aug. Müller (in *Königsberger Studien*, i. 1887). He takes the *stichoi* as the basis of his arrangement, and finds that the first part of the Song (*vv.* 1–6) and the last part (*vv.* 16–31) follow a regular stichical scheme, while in the middle (*vv.* 7–15) the structure becomes disturbed and irregular. In the first part the order of *stichoi* is 2. 4. 4. 2 (*v.* 2 has two members, *v.* 3 has four, and so on), and in the last part the order is 2. 4. 2. He notices further that, in a four-membered verse, the two subdivisions of each pair (i. e. of clauses *a* and *b*) are closely parallel in meaning, while clause *a* is not in complete parallelism with clause *b*, but the latter marks an advance in the thought upon the former. This scheme, according to Müller, furnishes the key to all the difficulties of the Song, and to the true restoration of the Text. It is remarkable that just where the structure becomes irregular there the obscurities of the Text begin (*vv.* 7–15). All goes smoothly before and after this central crux, the sequence of thought is natural, the style unbroken and correct. Accordingly Müller gives up these unfortunate verses as hopeless. 'The irregularity of the structure and of the order of thought, the difficulty of the language through clumsy attempts at correction, shew that this middle portion has been distorted until it can no longer be understood.' But it is doubtful whether the case is so bad as Müller

tries to make out. It is possible to extract sufficient sense
from these middle verses, though no doubt the Text has suffered. Rather than dislocate the Song as Müller proposes,
and assign the verses to another poet, it seems more reason-
able to suppose that the Text was difficult to begin with, and
that succeeding transcribers, through misunderstanding and
attempts at correction, only made matters worse. Moreover,
Müller's scheme does not always work even in the first
and last parts. For instance, in order to secure a two-mem-
bered verse between 3 and 4 he proposes to write 3ᵃ in four
members, and to make 3ᵇ the surviving limb of the missing
half-verse, in spite of the parallelism between אשירה and אמרה.
At the same time, in the working out of his ingenious theory,
Müller suggests certain corrections of the Text which we
shall gladly make use of.

On the whole, then, these attempts to arrange the Song in
anything more than a general division into obvious strophes,
however successful they may be to a certain extent, seem to
break down at the crucial points.

A characteristic of the poetical form of this Song is the
recurrence of the kind of parallelism known as the climactic
or progressive. Of this there are two classes: (1) cases where
the first line is *incomplete,* and the second line repeats some
words from it and completes them, e. g. 4ᵇ. 7. 12ᵃ. 19ᵃ. 23ᵇ; cf.
ψ. 29, 1. 89, 51. 92, 9ᵃ. 93, 3. 94, 3. 113, 1.   (2) where the
first line is *complete,* and the second repeats some words of it
with an addition, e. g. 3ᵇ. 5. 11 a β. 21. 24; cf. ψ. 22, 4. 29, 5.
8. 67, 3. 77, 16. Ex. 15, 16ᵇ; cf. *vv.* 4. 11. 14. This kind of
parallelism is uncommon, and belongs only to the most
elevated poetry.

1. ותשר דבורה וברק] This verse forms a title to the
Song, attached to it at a later age, and embodying the view of
posterity that Deborah (if not Barak as well) was the com-
poser and the singer of the poem. Perhaps Barak was

inserted in the title on the strength of the apostrophe in
v. 12, and it was supposed that he and Deborah sang the ode
antiphonally, though there is nothing either in the form or
in the contents to support the idea. That Deborah was the
authoress and singer was concluded, no doubt, from *vv.* 3. 7.
12. 13. At first sight it looks as if the first pers. in *vv.* 3 and
13 could refer to no other than Deborah; but against this
must be set the fact that the prophetess herself is mentioned
by name, and wherever her name occurs it is in connexion
with the second (*vv.* 7 see note, 12) or third person (*v.*
15). In fact Deborah and Barak are addressed by name
in *v.* 12; they could hardly address a summons to themselves.
Therefore some other explanation must be found for the
occurrence of the first person in the Song. The patriot poet
may well be imagined to have acted as the mouthpiece of his
victorious countrymen, and to represent their feelings in an
ode of thanksgiving. There are abundant analogies to justify
this view. Elsewhere a single tribe or the entire community
speaks in 'terms properly applicable only to an individual;'
e.g. the tribe of Judah in 1, 3; the בני ישראל in 20, 23; the
איש ישראל in Josh. 9, 7, and the בני יוסף in 17, 14 f. 17 f. JE;
Moses and the children of Israel in Ex. 15, 1. 2; cf. Num. 20,
18. 19 JE with Dt. 2, 27–29; 'this custom is due, probably,
partly to a sense of community of interests and sympathies
pervading the entire group, partly to the love of personifi-
cation' (Driver, *Introduction*, p. 366).

ביום ההוא] The Redactor's expression in 4, 23.

2. ב...ברכו] 'on account of ... bless ye.' This construction does not occur again; Gen. 12, 3. 18, 18. 28, 4
ונברכו בך being hardly parallel. For ב in this sense, cf. Gen.
18, 28 בחמשה, and בגלל, באשר etc.

פרע פרעות] The primary meaning of the root seems to
be *to loosen.* In the O.T. it denotes *let loose:* (1) in a
general sense, e.g. Ex. 5, 4 J; *to cast off restraint,* Ex. 32, 25 E.
Ezra 24, 14; in Prov., *to set at nought* counsel etc. 1, 25. 4; 15
etc. (with accus.), 8, 33 (absol.). (2) In a special sense, of
letting the hair go loose, forbidden to the priests, Lev. 10, 6.
21, 10, commanded in the case of a leper Lev. 13, 45, of a

woman suspected of adultery Num. 5, 18, and of a Nazarite
Num. 6, 5.

But this meaning *to loosen* in connexion with the hair does
not help us here, nor in Dt. 32, 42 מראש פרעות אויב. In order
to find a sense for these two passages we must suppose that
the root-meaning was developed thus ; to loosen oneself from
something, to become separate, prominent, and so a leader,
chief. Thus we may render here, ' for the leading of the
leaders,' and the place in Dt., 'from the head (i. e. chief) of the
leaders of the enemy.' In Arabic the verb فرع primarily seems
to = *he* or *it overtopped* or *surpassed in height; he was superior,
excelled*. Derivatives of the root are used of the top of a
mountain, of a mountain high above the surrounding land.
In Targ. Onk. Dt. 16, 18 and Jon. Ex. 20, 5 שטרים = פורענים.

The rendering given above is supported by LXX. Α. Luc. Θ.
Syr.-Hex. ἐν τῷ ἄρξασθαι ἀρχηγούς. So in Dt. l. c. ἀπὸ κεφαλῆς
ἀρχόντων ἐχθρῶν. Cod. B renders ἀπεκαλύφθη ἀποκάλυμμα,
also Σ. ἐν τῷ ἀνακαλύψασθαι, as in other places where this root
occurs—e. g. Lev. 13, 45 (10, 6. 21, 10 according to some
codd.). Num. 5, 18. Dt. 32, 42 Σ. The Pesh. has ܟ̈ܒܘ̈ܣܬܐ
ܕܐܬܠ̱ܝ = ' for the vengeance which the . . . took,' according
to the common usage of the word in the Targums ; so Arab.
Vulg., qui sponte obtulistis de Isr. animas vestras, etc.

Another rendering has been suggested, based upon the use
of the word in reference to the long hair of the Nazarites ;
' for the loosing of the hairs,' i.e. ' for those whose hair was
let flow loose,' i.e. the Nazarites, the devoted men (like
Samson and Samuel) who had let their hair grow long, and
so had received the supernatural force through which the
enemy was routed. Maurice Vernes, *Revue des Études juives*,
Jan.–Mar. 1892, reviving an old explanation dating from
Cassel.

Perhaps the words might be used as synonyms for ardent
and consecrated service, but the first rendering seems safer.

פרעות] lit. *leadings ;* fem. plur. because abstract instead
of concrete; cf. כנות Ezra 4, 7, and אבות. For the fem. cf.
Arab. ḥalifa, etc., Ges.-Kautzsch, § 122. 4. b and *n*.

בהתנדב עם] Cf. *v.* 9. The Hithp. occurs again twelve

times, all in Chr., Ezra, and Nehem., generally of donations offered to the Temple (1 C. 29, 5. 6. 9. 14. 17. Ezra 1, 6 etc.); in 2 C. 17, 16 of consecration with a view to military service. This may be the meaning here, though the rendering, 'self-offering of the people,' gives a sense more suitable to the antiquity of the Song. Illustr. from ψ. 110, 3 עַמְּךָ נְדָבוֹת. LXX. ἐν τῷ ἀκουσιασθῆναι λαόν Bℵ. ἐν προαιρέσει λαοῦ A. Luc. Θ. Syr.-Hex. Orig. ἐν ἑκουσιασμῷ λαοῦ 'A.

3. מְלָכִים] . . . רֹזְנִים] Together, as in ψ. 2, 2. Pr. 8, 15. 31, 4. Hab. 1, 10. cf. Pr. 14, 28.   An invitation (hardly ironical, Reuss) to the surrounding chiefs, Canaanite and others, to attend the praises of the victorious God of Israel.   For רֹזְנִים LXX. has σατράπαι.

אָנֹכִי לי' אָנֹכִי] For the suspended pronoun אָנֹכִי ' *I*—to Yahweh *I* will sing,' cf. Gen. 37, 30ᵇ. ψ. 76, 8. Driver, *Tenses*, § 198. Obs. 2.   LXX. Bℵ. ἐγώ εἰμι τῷ Κυρίῳ ἐγώ εἰμι ᾄσομαι.

4. בְּצֵעְדְּךָ] denotes stately movement.   Of Jehovah only again in Hab. 3, 12 and ψ. 68, 8, both borrowing from this place; ? Is. 63, 1 (Cheyne).

גַם . . . גַם] Cf. Job 15, 10.

נָטְפוּ] Cf. ψ. 68, 9.   Budde suggests נָמוֹטוּ or נָמוֹגוּ, but these verbs are used of the earth, hills, mountains, foundations of the earth, not of the heavens.   The use of נָטְפוּ here can be quite well accounted for by the principle of the parallelism explained above (p. 27).   Vulg. om.

נָטְפוּ מַיִם] For the accus. after a verb of abounding, over-flowing, cf. Joel 4, 18 יִטְּפוּ הֶהָרִים עָסִיס.   Ges. § 117. 4. 4 *b*.

5. נָזְלוּ] for נָזֹלּוּ Is. 63, 19. 64, 2, imitated from here; nif. pf. of זלל=*shake, tremble*. Cf. Gen. 11, 7. Ezek. 41, 7. Ges. § 67. 11, for the weakened pronunciation. LXX. ἐσαλεύθησαν. Pesh. ܙܥ. This agrees with the parallel רָעֲשָׁה. The Mass., Kimchi, etc. took it from נזל=*flow*. Vulg. fluxerunt. So Ew. In Mic. 1, 4. ψ. 97, 5 we find הָרִים . . . נָמַסּוּ.

זֶה סִינַי] The demonstrative here is to be taken rather as emphasizing the following subs. than as used δεικτικῶς, ' Sinai indeed,' 'Sinai I say,' not 'yon Sinai.' So Is. 23, 13. ψ. 104, 25. In the same way זֹה is used adverbially to strengthen an interrogative. Ges.-Kau. § 136. 2 *n*.

The question here arises, do these two verses describe the coming down of Jehovah from Edom and Sinai to help in the battle, or do they allude to the Theophany which took place at the Exodus? Wellh., *Prolegomena*, p. 359, says that Sinai was looked upon as the dwelling-place of Jehovah, from which He issued on different occasions to help Israel, and to place Himself at the head of His warriors in their battles. So Reuss, in loc.; Rob. Smith, *Prophets*, p. 34, *Religion of Semites*, p. 111. The Godhead descends in storm and thunder, in the very storm which did so much to win the battle, see *vv.* 13. 20 f. This was a common conception among the ancient Israelites, and no doubt may be traced back to a reminiscence of that stupendous Theophany which inaugurated Israel's existence as a nation. Similar accompaniments of Jehovah's manifestation are described or expected in ψ. 18, 8–16. 50, 3. 97, 2. 3. Mic. 1, 3. 4. Is. 64, 1 ff. 29, 6. But in this passage there is an important element which differentiates the Theophany described here from those just enumerated, and that is the mention of Edom and Sinai. Now whenever either of these places is named in connexion with a manifestation of the Godhead, the reference is always to the great revelation of Jehovah at the Exodus (Ex. 19). See Dt. 33, 2. Hab. 3, 3 ff. ψ. 68, 7. 8. cf. 77, 17–19. After-ages came to look back upon this epoch-making event, when Jehovah came down to give His law to His people and lead them into their promised land, as a pledge of His continued presence and help in times of difficulty. This is the case here. The poet calls upon his victorious countrymen to praise Jehovah, who had in former days declared Himself to be the God of Israel by a special revelation, and marched to the assistance of His chosen tribes. He has once again proved Himself to be Israel's Protector and Deliverer. It is to be observed that in these verses Jehovah comes from Edom, and Sinai trembles before Him. This must mean that He comes from Edom to Sinai; He does not come from Edom (or Sinai) to the field of battle. And further, in the other Theophanies the mighty effects of Jehovah's presence appear at once in the overthrow of His enemies, and in the deliverance of His faithful ones. But here there is

a wide interval before the account of the battle in *vv.* 20 ff.
Accordingly we conclude that the reference here is to the past
revelation at Sinai. So Bertheau, Hilliger, Ewald (*Dichter
d. A. B.*, p. 188), etc. Recently, Robertson, *Early Religion of
Israel*, 1892, pp. 193 ff.

It is to be observed that Jehovah's progress moves along
from Edom, that is from the north, to Sinai. From the
same quarter comes the Theophany in Ezek. 1, 4 ff. Thus we
seem to find here a trace of the old mythological idea that the
ever-mysterious north was the peculiar home of deity, Is. 14,
13 ; cf. Job 37, 22 and Ezek. 25, 13. 14. See also Lev. 1, 11 ;
the victim is to be slain towards the north, before Jehovah.
According to one conception, then, Jehovah's dwelling-place
was in Edom (so Hab. l.c., Paran, cf. Is. 63, 1), according to
the other it was at Sinai, and the Theophany moves over
Seir and Paran on the way to Kadesh, Dt. 33.

6. שמגר] Only again in 3, 31.

יעל] Bertheau, enlarging on the difficulty of identifying
יעל here with the heroine of *vv.* 24 ff., supposes that there was
a judge of this name, otherwise unknown. It is simpler to
suppose either that the poet names the two most famous
characters of the age, both of whom brought deliverance from
the prevailing distress, or that the words בימי יעל must be
struck out as a gloss crept in from the margin. Bickell,
p. 196 *n.*, is willing to do this.

חדלו] *ceased, kept holiday,* i.e. were unfrequented. LXX.
ἐξέλιπον ὁδούς B. ἐξέλειπον βασιλεῖς A. Luc. Syr.-Hex., prob.
through some confusion with 7ᵃ.

עקלקלוך] For the redupl. form, cf. חֲלַקְלַקּוֹת, אֲדַמְדָּם, יְרַקְרַק.
Stade, *Lehrbuch*, § 234 a. For other forms from this root, see
Is. 27, 1. Hab. 1, 4. ψ. 125, 5.

ילכו] Impf. frequentative, here followed by accus. of place,
as in Dt. 1, 19. Job 29, 3. Is. 57, 2. Ew., *Syntax*, § 282 a.

7. פרזון and פרזונו *v.* 11] The exact form is not found
again. The other derivatives of the root are used in two
ways: (1) of open villages situated on the plain, as opposed to
lofty, fortified towns ; the best illustration is Ezek. 38, 11 ; cf.
1 S. 6, 18. Zech. 2, 8. Esth. 9, 19 ; (2) of the inhabitants of

these unwalled villages, living sometimes on the lower plains,
sometimes in the hill-country, called the פְרָזוֹי, often mentioned
among the tribes of Canaan, Gen. 13, 20, etc. But neither
of these meanings is suitable here. The nearest parallel is the
use of the word in Hab. 3, 14 פְרָזָו רֹאשׁ בְּמַטָּיו נָקַבְתָּ, 'warriors,'
R.V., 'hordes' or 'villages,' R.V.M. The Verss. throw some
light on the meaning, v. 7. LXX. ἐξέλιπον δυνατοί B. ἐξέλιπον φραζών A. Luc. Some codd. οἱ κατοικοῦντες; so Vet. Lat.
Vulg., fortes, so v. 11. Pesh. ܦܨܝܚܐ ('level tracts').
Targ. קוּרֵי פַצְחָיא ('villages'), so v. 11; cf. Zech. 2, 4 Targ.
In Hab. 3, 14 LXX. has δυναστῶν 'A. Σ. In v. 11 LXX.
δικαιοσύνας αὔξησον B. δ'. ἐνίσχυσαν A. δίκαιοι ἐνίσχυσαν Luc.
φραζών 'A. ἀτείχιστοι Σ. ἐνίσχυσον Θ. Pesh. ܙܕܝܩܘܗܝ.

Thus the Versions understood the word to mean 'powerful,' 'strong,' etc. The LXX. of Ezek. 38, 11. Esth. 9, 19,
recognizes the meaning 'scatter, separate.' The root idea
was probably 'separation,' and so 'eminence, power, leading.'
Like פְרָעוֹת v. 2 the word is used as an abstract. So translate
in v. 7 *the rulers ceased*, and in v. 11 *the righteous acts of his
rule*, subj. gen. as the preceding צִדְקוֹת ייׇ shews. The meaning
must surely be the same in both verses; 'villages' might
suit v. 7 but not v. 11, and so must be abandoned, although
Budde is in favour of retaining it for v. 7.

שַׁקַּמְתִּי] One Babyl. cod. has שָׂ, two old Edns. and a few
MSS. have שָ; cf. 6, 17 שָׁאָפָה, and Cant. 1, 7. Job 19, 29? It
is remarkable to find this form of the relative, generally
characteristic of the later language, in a writing of the
antiquity of the Song. It occurs, however, doubtfully in two
old documents, Gen. 6, 3. 49, 10 J, and may perhaps be a
peculiarity of the N. Palestinian dialect (Stade, *Lehrb.*, § 10ᵇ),
e. g. 7, 12. 8, 26. Cant. 1, 7–12. 4, 20. The antiquity of the
form has been recently confirmed by the discovery of a small
weight, prob. of the 8th cent., on the site of Samaria, bearing
the inscription רבע של רבע נצג. Neubauer, *Athenæum*, Aug. 2,
1890.

קמתי] was no doubt originally intended to be a 2nd fem.
sing. (see v. 12), the old ending in -*ti* being preserved, as in
Jer. 2, 20 (*bis*). Mic. 4, 13. Grätz, Wellh., Reuss, Müller, etc.

D

Ges. § 44. 2. 4 *n*. The Mass. evidently took it as 1st pers., otherwise there would have been a Q^{e}ri, as in Ruth 3, 3. 4 שָׁכָבְתִּי, יָרַדְתִּי. Jer. 2, 33. 3, 5. See Wright, *Compar. Gr.*, p. 173. LXX. Luc. Vu. 3rd pers.; Pe. Targ. 1st pers.

אם בישראל] Cf. use of אם in Is. 22, 21. Job 29, 16. Also Gen. 45, 8 E.

The mention of Deborah's 'arising' to deliver her people, before the description of the previous distress is completed, creates a difficulty. We should expect 7^c to come after *v.* 8, or, as Meier places it, after *v.* 9. The poet carries us back to the unhappy days of Shamgar; but before they are over he suddenly introduces us to another and a later age, that of Deborah; and then goes back to Shamgar's days again, *v.* 8. He proceeds to heighten his description of Israel's helplessness, and records the free self-offering of the leaders, for which he would have men 'bless Jehovah.' And then, to our surprise, Deborah is summoned to 'awake' (*v.* 12) after she has already 'arisen' in *v.* 7^c. Müller lays stress upon this irregularity as a proof of the disturbed and corrupt state of the middle part of the Song (pp. 18. 19). Budde would strike out 7^c as being a gloss, shewn to be such by its illogical position, and by the recurrence of שׁ; he would take the second חדלו as the remainder of the original third member of the verse. On the other hand, we cannot expect in an ode like this, so full of eager and exultant emotion, to find the order of events and the order of thought always arranged in strict sequence. It is not unusual in Hebrew writing to find an author describing the issue of a series of events by anticipation, and then returning to give the further particulars, which, logically, should have been given before; e. g. Gen. 37, 6 and 5^b. 42, 21 ff. and 20. Jud. 6, 27, etc. See Driver, *Tenses*, § 75. So there does not seem sufficient reason for altering the text here.

Bickell (*Supplem.*) omits חדלו^2 and שׁקמתי^2 for metrical reasons. He says that many of the repetitions in the Song were inserted for the purposes of singing and musical accompaniment.

8. יבחר אלהים חדשים] This most difficult expression has been explained in three ways: (1) Taking Israel (under-

stood) as the subj., 'they chose new gods.' Then the meaning, taken with the context, will be, 'Isr. was unfaithful to Jehovah ; he preferred to serve the gods of the neighbouring people, and consequently he was punished with the sufferings inflicted by his enemies.' LXX. ἐξελέξαντο θεοὺς καινούς Bℵ. ἡρέτισαν θ΄. κενούς A*. καινούς Luc. Θ. Syr.-II. Targ. Cf. Dt. 32, 17. Jud. 10, 14—both later than this Song.

This would be quite in accordance with the theory of the Redactor, but it would hardly come from the author of the Song. Moreover, at the time when the Song was written, the idea prevailed, as it did down to a much later period, that to adopt the deity and cult of a neighbouring people was equivalent to entering into a close alliance with that people ; therefore if Israel 'chose' the gods of the Canaanites the consequence would have been friendship, not war, between them. There is nothing in the description of the distress in *vv.* 6. 7 to suggest that it was due to national apostasy.

(2) Ewald, followed by Bertheau and others, takes Israel as the subject, but renders אלהים *judges.* For אלהים signifying a judge as the *mouthpiece of the Divine sentence,* see Ex. 21, 6. 22, 7 f. 27 J, and cf. 18, 16. 19. 1 S. 2, 25. This would give good sense ; in the time of oppression they 'chose new judges' to resist the enemy and deliver the sufferers. In this case the following clause will mean exactly the opposite from what it did above ; 'under the leadership of the new judge attacks were made on the *enemy's* gates.' The great objection to this explanation is that the undoubted use of אלהים for *judge* is practically confined to the Book of the Covenant (refs. above), that is to say, in a context which is concerned with legal decisions and naturally suggests this meaning. But here it is quite different. Elohim would not be the word used for a judge in the sense required here, a warrior and deliverer. As Bissinger says (quoted by Hilliger, p. 29), when 'judges' or 'leaders' occur in the Song other expressions are used (*vv.* 2. 7. 9. 14. 15) ; and אלהים here would lead to inevitable mis- understanding.

(3) Making אלהים the subject, 'God chose new things.' Pesh. Arab. Bar-Heb. Vulg., nova bella elegit Dominus.

The obvious objections to this are, that יהוה is always the name of the Deity in the Song, and where אלהים does occur it is in the phrase יהוה אלהי ישראל (*vv.* 3. 5); 'new things' would be not חדשים but the fem. חדשות, as in Is. 42, 9. 48, 6 or חדשה Is. 43, 19. Jer. 31, 21.

The fact is, nothing can be made out of the text as it stands: there must be an ancient corruption here, but it is too deep-seated for emendation (but see Budde, below, on next cl.). Perhaps an early attempt was made at correcting the passage from Dt. 32, 17; and this must have become stereotyped as part of the text before the Greek Version was made.

יבחר] If right, the impf. here vividly conjures up the past; cf. *vv.* 26. 29. Driver, *Tenses,* § 27 a.

אז לחם שערים] If, as seems most probable, this verse continues the description of the unsettled times before Deborah, then אז must refer to some occasion in that period when a sally was made against the enemy's gates. It was a bold attempt to throw off the enemy's oppressive yoke, but it proved unsuccessful. The Israelite army, though its full strength numbered 40,000 men, had been rendered ineffective through the loss of proper weapons; not a shield or a spear was to be seen among them, they were forced to arm themselves with such rude implements as they could find. A deliverer who should win an effectual victory was yet to come.

לָחֶם] The Mass. specially notes it as milraʻ, *Ochla Wᵉ Ochla,* 373, in a list of words usually with the accent on the penultima, but exceptionally accented on the ultima; that is to say, it was taken as a pausal form of לֶחֶם. Cf. for seghol in final accented shut syll. (in pause) מָצֶחָק Gen. 21, 9. Ex. 32, 6. Dt. 32, 11. Kimchi explains it as a Qal form like יָבֵשׁ, with seghol for çere (*Rad. Lib.* s. v.). It is probably an Infin. Piel used as a noun, cf. פַּלֵּט ψ. 32, 7. נַפֵּץ Dan. 12, 7 (both doubtful). The Piel of לחם does not occur again; the form must be pronounced very uncertain.

לחם שערים] Lit. 'battle of, i. e. at, the gates.' For this obj. gen. cf. 1 K. 18, 19 אכלי שלחן איזבל. ψ. 69, 13. Ges. § 128. 2 b. As *v.* 11 shews, the 'gates' must be those of the enemy.

LXX. ὅτε ἐπολέμησαν πόλεις ἀρχόντων B. ἀρχ'. probably only an explanatory addition. The Vulg. explicitly renders, portas hostium ipse subvertit. But LXX. A. Luc. point the words לָחֶם שְׂעֹרִים, and render ὡς ἄρτον κρίθινον. So Pesh. Arab.; V. L. Elegerunt ut panem hordaceum deos novos: tunc expugnaverunt civitates principum; so some Greek codd. Following this punctuation Budde suggests as an emendation for clause ᵃ, וּבְחִי אֱלֹהִים חֲדָשִׁים אוֹ לָחֶם שְׂעֹרִים, i. e. 'The sacrifices of God came only on the new moons, then was there barley bread' and nothing better—a further mark of the distress of the time; sacrifices could be offered, i. e. meat could be eaten, only once a month! This does not commend itself.

יֵרָאֶה] Impf. used of past time in an interrog. sentence; *was there ever . . to be seen . . ?* cf. Gen. 43, 7 נֵדַע. חִידוּע. 2 S. 3, 33. Driver, *Tenses,* § 39 β.

LXX. θυρεὸς ἐὰν ὀφθῇ καὶ λόγχη B. σκέπη νεανίδων σιρομαστῶν· ἀνήφθη καὶ σιρομαστής A. σκ'. νε'. ἂν ὀφθῇ καὶ σειρομαστής Luc. σκ'. νε'. σειρομαστῶν Θ. The rend. of the three latter forms of the Gk. Vers. is curious. Theodoret gives the reading ἐὰν ἴδω σειρομαστῶν τεσσ. χιλ.; hence Field ingeniously conjectures that the reading of A. Luc. Θ. νεανίδων arose out of ἐὰν ἴδω. Thus ἀνήφθη A. ἂν ὀφθῇ Luc. becomes a double rendering of יראה, and καὶ στρομαστής an insertion to fill up the sense. The Vulg. and Pesh. follow the M. T.

9. After לִבִּי supply 'saith,' 'leans.' חוּקְקֵי Qal ptcp. with 3rd rad. preserved instead of being assimilated. Cf. Is. 10, 1. 22, 16. ψ. 8, 3 etc. Stade, *Lehrb.,* § 105. The meaning here is 'leaders' rather than 'lawgivers;' Qal ptcp. only here in this sense, cf. v. 14.

LXX. τὰ διατεταγμένα τῷ Ἰσραήλ Luc. Orig. τὰ προστάγματα Σ. τοῖς ἀκριβαζομένοις Ἀ. Θ.; the three latter render similarly מחקק in Gen. 49, 10. Vulg., principes. Pesh. ܡܚܩܩܐ = *interpreter,* Arab. The Pesh. uses this word for מחקק in v. 14. Gen. 49, 10. Dt. 33, 21. Is. 33, 22; prob. a free translation, for in ψ. 60, 9. 108, 9 מחקק is rendered ܡܠܟܝ *my king.*

הַמִּתְנַדְּבִים] see v. 2. LXX. οἱ ἑκουσιαζόμενοι ἐν λαῷ B. οἱ δυνάσται τοῦ λαοῦ A. Luc. Syr.-Hex. The poet has summoned the patriot leaders to praise Jehovah; now other classes of

the community are called upon to take their share in cele-
brating the victory.

10. צחרות אתנות רכבי] *ye that ride on white she-asses.*
The root צחר only occurs again in the pr. name צֹחַר and in
Ezek. 27, 18 צָחַר צֶמֶר. The meaning of the word must be
sought from the Arab. صَهَرَ = *to wither, become yellow* or
brown, اِصْهَارّ of a plant (Lane). But primarily the root = *to
burn*, of the sun; hence of a colour produced by the burning
sunlight, brown, or reddish-yellow, صُهْبَة *ânesses roussâtres*
(Reuss), not 'dazzling white' as Ges. *Thes.* See Müller,
Königsb. Studien, pp. 5 f. The old Israelite chiefs used to ride
on asses, just as the members of the ruling house in Zanzibar,
and as the schêchs in S. Arabia do at the present day. See
10, 4. 12, 14. 2 S. 17, 23. 19, 27.

LXX. ἐπιβεβηκότες ἐπὶ ὄνου θηλείας μεσημβρίας (צהרים) B.
ἐπιβ. ἐπὶ ὑποζυγίων A. Luc. + ἐπιλαμπηνῶν. Thus A. does not
transl. צחורות. Some codd. have μεσημβρίας καὶ λαμπουσῶν.
Syr.-Hex. στιλβουσῶν Σ. Pesh. Vulg. as M. T.

מדין על ישבי] *ye that sit upon saddle-cloths* or *carpets.*
The root מדד = *extend, measure out*, and so מַד (plur. מַדִּים)=
usually a *garment* (3, 16. 1 S. 4, 12 etc. Lev. 6, 3. ψ. 133, 2),
but here the reference must be to the garments, i. e. saddle-
cloths, of the asses. Illustr. fr. Ezek. 27, 20 בגדי חפש לרכבה.
The context shews that those referred to by ישבי must be
riding, moving in procession. מדין, Aram. plur. ending, Ges.
§ 87. 1 a. ? North Palestinian.

LXX. καθημένοι ἐπὶ κριτηρίου B. Luc. (i. e. מן and דין);
Targ. Vulg. καθημένοι ἐπὶ λαμπηνῶν (=*chariots*) A, cf. 1 K.
26, 5. 7. Is. 66, 20 LXX. The Pesh. freely, *in houses.*

על ישבי] Constr. st. before prepos., cf. Is. 9, 1. ψ. 2, 13 etc.;
Ew., *Syntax*, § 289 b.

דרך על והלכי] LXX. καὶ πορευόμενοι ἐπὶ ὁδοὺς συνέδρων
ἐφ᾽ ὁδῷ (a doublet) B. A omits. καὶ π᾽. ἐφ᾽ ὁδῷ Luc. Pesh. Vulg.

שיחו] The verb is used in the O. T. as follows: (1) *to
speak*, e. g. ψ. 69, 13. Job 7, 11. 12, 8 etc. (2) *to speak to
oneself*, ψ. 77, 7 לבבי עם. Gen. 24, 63 J, so *to meditate*, ψ. 105, 2.
119, 15 etc., and, with the nuance of meditating sadly,
ψ. 55, 18. 77, 4. Similarly the noun; (1) *talk*, 2 K. 9, 11.

(2) *troubled speech, complaint,* 1 S. 1, 16. ψ. 55, 3 and oft. in Job.
(3) *thought, meditation,* Am. 4, 13. 1 K. 18, 27. Job 15, 4.
Thus the word never=*to sing,* Bertheau, etc., and it is commonly used only in late books. Its rare occurrence in earlier literature does not warrant more than the transl., *muse, meditate.* This would hardly be forcible enough to suit the exultant tone of the context. Can the word be right? If it is corrupt, it must have reached its present form before the LXX. transl. was made, as is the case with other corruptions in the Song. LXX. has διηγεῖσθε B. φθέγξασθαι A. Luc. Syr.-Hex. ὁμιλεῖτε 'A. φθέγξασθε Σ. Pesh. ܐܘܝ. All the Verss., except Vulg., loquimini, attach the word to the foll. verse; but the contraction מן שיח is never found; the verb always takes ב, or ל, or an accus. It is difficult to find a satisfactory emendation. One might suggest שמחו; or better שמעו, cancelling the מ at the beginning of the following word, ... *listen! The shout of the archers ...!* But there would be the objection that the copyist could hardly have misunderstood such a simple word as שמעו and allowed it to become שיחו.

11. מקול מחצצים בין משאבים] The prep. creates a difficulty. After *from the voice ...* we might expect to have the sentence completed with some such phrase as, 'let praise be heard' (Ber., edn. 1, Keil, Cheyne). All kinds of meanings have been forced upon this awkward מן, 'away from,' 'louder than,' 'with.' Bertheau in his last edn. renders 'on account of,' 'by reason of the shout ... let men rehearse ...' cf. Is. 6, 4. 24, 18. 31, 4. Jer. 3, 9. ψ. 55, 4; the shout of the archers, now resting after victory, is to be an impulse for general thanksgiving. But in the examples which Ber. quotes the meaning of מן is made clear by the construction of the verb immediately before or after it, while here שם יתנו must begin a fresh sentence, and שם cannot introduce the apodosis. Either a clause has dropped out, or, more probably, מ did not originally belong to קול (Budde); the מ of מדין above, or the מ at the beginning of the following word may have caught the copyist's eye and led him to write the letter here by mistake. If it is removed an excellent sense results, *Hark! the archers ...!* or, *The shout of the archers ...!*

מחצצים] Probably a denominative of חץ *an arrow;* so Jewish interpreters, Kimchi יורי החצים, Luth., Schult., and most moderns.   Ewald compares Pr. 30, 27 חצץ and Arab. خَصَّ = *make a line,* subs. = *a line,* and rends. 'those who keep time' on musical instruments, cf. LXX.   A third rendering is *those who divide,* scil. the spoil, making חצה = חצין.   But it is too much to supply such an obj. as 'spoil,' and חלק is the proper word (*v.* 30).

Budde conjectures מצחקים, and translates, 'Hark, how merry they are . . . !'   But there is more colour and force in the text as it is.

משאבים] The verb always means *to draw water;* the noun (only here) with prefixed מ will consequently = *places for drawing water* (Ges. § 85, 48), or *water-troughs.*   LXX. ὑδρευομένων B.   The cool, shaded wells are a common place of rendezvous in the East.   There parties of victorious archers were resting after the battle.

The Verss. present great varieties of rendering.   LXX. [διηγεῖσθε] ἀπὸ φωνῆς ἀνακρουομένων (= pulsantes, 'beating musical instruments,' cf. 1 C. 25, 5, חוה LXX.) ἀνὰ μέσον ὑδρευομένων B. [φθέγξασθαι] φωνήν ἀνακρ'. ἀνὰ μεσ'. εὐφραιρομένων A. Luc. Syr.-Hex.   For ὑδρ'., 'A has καταλεγόντων. Σ συμπινόντων (i. e. מסבאים fr. סבא *potavit,* cf. Nah. 1, 10 Σ). 'A.'s rendering cannot be traced to any Hebrew word.   Pesh. ܐܬܗܓܘ ܒܡ̈ܠܐ ܕܒܨܝܐ ܥܡ [ܘ], i.e. 'consider the words of the investigators (cf. Is. 23, 13 Pesh. = ἐκζητηται Bar. 3, 23) who are among the learned'—a curious paraphrase ; so Arab. Vulg., ubi collisi sunt currus, et hostium suffocatus est exercitus. Targ. understands מחצצים as something to do with robbers, בית מכונת לסתין, and explains משאבים as a בית שקיא, 'the place where the sons of Israel went to fill water.'

שם יתנו צדקות י"י] *there let men rehearse the righteous acts of Jehovah.*   יתנו vb. only again in this sense, 11, 40.   Arab. تَنَّى Conj. iv. = *praise;* תנה in Aram. = *announce.*   The meaning here is a combination of both.   In Hos. 8, 9. 10 Hif. of תנה = *hire,* whence אתנן, אתנה.

צדקות י"י] Jehovah here is the subj. genit.   For the expression cf. Mic. 6, 5. 1 S. 12, 7. ψ. 103, 6.

צֶד' פְּרוֹזְנוֹ] This must also be subj. genit.: 'The righteous acts of His rule in Israel.' See on *v.* 7.

אָז יֵרְדוּ וְגוֹ'] There has been a good deal of dispute as to the significance of אז in the Song. Ew. (*Dichter d. A.B.*, p. 184) treats it, together with ירד (here and *v.* 13), as a 'kriegerischer Ausdruck,' and wherever it occurs (*vv.* 8. 11. 13. 19. 22) he understands it as referring to the battle and the victory. So Bertheau. This, however, seems to force the context into an *à priori* uniformity. The poet deliberately avoids the more regular method of marking the succession of events, and chooses a particle which enables him to express more vividly his intense realization of the past, and to emphasize each particular feature in his description. At one time אז is associated with an impf. which calls up the more distant days before Deborah (*v.* 8), at another time it is preceded by imperatives (*v.* 12), commonly it stands in connexion with a perfect (*vv.* 11. 13. 19. 22). Its meaning, then, is determined in each case by the context, sometimes, as in *vv.* 8. 19. and 22, by the foregoing verb; cf. for use of אז in poetry Gen. 49, 4. Ex. 15, 15. Is. 33, 23. ψ. 2, 5. 96, 12 etc.

שְׁעָרִים] Obviously, the 'gates' of the enemy; because ירד in the Song is always used of the march of the Israelite army to the battle, *vv.* 13. 14.

It is difficult to find a suitable connexion between these words and the previous part of the verse. Clause [a] gives a picture of the victorious soldiery resting after battle, and bids them recapitulate with thanksgiving Jehovah's deeds for His people. Then clause [b] begins a description of the campaign. But as we have seen (p. 24 f.) the main break in the Song occurs here, and *v.* 12 serves as the prelude to Part ii, introducing the real subject of the ode. Accordingly 11[b] anticipates in an awkward fashion the description of the battle which is to follow. It presents a striking likeness to the first part of *v.* 13, and it is more than probable that this clause is a doublet of the latter, incorrectly inserted here. Budde is in favour of this view. If 11[b] is struck out, the rhythm and balance of the verse will be greatly improved.

Vulg. has a paraphrastic addition : tunc descendit ad portas populus Domini, et obtinuit principatum.

12. עוּרִי] So accented for sake of emphasis in earnest and vigorous speech : cf. Is. 51, 9. Zech. 13, 7. See Hupf.- Nowack on ψ. 3, 8 (foot-note).

דברי] E. Meier (*Uebersetzung u. Erkl. d. Debora-Liedes*, Tüb. 1859, p. 38) supposes that there is a play here on the name דבורה. This may be so. He renders, ' Lead the song.' This might possibly be the meaning of Hif. (Arab. Conj. iv. = *lead back*), but not of Piel. ' To lead' is the common meaning of the root in Aram.

וּשֶׁבַה] For the hatef-pathah cf. Lev. 25, 34 וּשָׂדֵה. Num. 23, 18 וּשֶׁמַע.

שֲׁבֵה שֶׁבִי] = *take prisoner* Num. 21, 1. 2 C. 28, 17, or *lead off a train of captives* Dt. 21, 10. ψ. 68, 19. But Luth., Wellh., Stade, Budde read שֹׁבֶיךָ *those who lead thee captive ;* cf. 1 K. 8, 46. 1 C. 6, 36 ; cf. Is. 14, 2.

LXX. A after Δεββώρα adds ἐξεγείρου μυριάδας μετὰ λαοῦ, so Luc. Similarly, instead of B's ἀνάστα Βαράκ A reads ἐνισχύων ἐξανάστασο Βαρὰχ καὶ ἐνίσχυσον Δεββωρὰ τὸν Βαράχ. Luc. has ἐξανιστὰς ὁ Βαρὰκ καὶ κατίσχυσον, Δεββωρὰ, τὸν Βαράκ ; so Syr.-Hex. The Pesh. Vulg. follow M. T.

13. יֵרַד is evidently intended by Mass. to be an apocopated impf. Piel of רדה (Ges. § 69. 1. c *n.*), with the meaning, ' Then shall the remnant (i. e. of Isr.) rule over the mighty ones.' But Piel of רדה does not occur, and אדירים like גבורים in clause [b] refers to Israelites. So point as perfect יָרַד = *went down.* LXX. κατέβη B א ; Pesh.

שָׂרִיד לָאַדִּירִים עָם] ' a remnant of the nobles (of the) people.' For שָׂרִיד ל cf. the construction מִזְמוֹר לְדָוִד. The M.T. takes עָם in appos. to אדירים (Vulg. Targ.). An alternative is to place the athnah at אדירים, and attach עָם to the beginning of the next clause ; ' the people of Jehovah came down for me with the heroes.' So LXX. B. This removes the awkwardness of the apposition, and would give a suitable parallelism with אדירים.

The Versions here are curious. LXX. τότε κατέβη κατάλημμα

τοῖς ἰσχυροῖς· λαὸς Κυρίου κατέβη αὐτῷ ἐν τοῖς κραταιοῖς ἐξ ἐμοῦ B. πότε ἐμεγάλυνεν ἡ ἰσχὺς αὐτοῦ· κε· ταπείνωσόν μοι τοὺς ἰσχυροτέρους μου A. ὁπότε ἐμεγαλύνθη κ.τ.λ. as A., Luc. Σ. has λείψανον and 'A. σωζομένοις for καταλ'. and ἰσχυροῖς; prob. both are interpretations of שׂריד. Pesh. takes this word as meaning 'saviour,' مخصﻟ; so Arab. Targ. somewhat similarly. Vulg., salvatae sunt reliquiae populi, Dominus in fortibus dimicavit.

'Then came down a remnant of the noble ones' must refer to the six tribes who alone, out of all Israel, rallied to the standard of Deborah and Barak. But אדירים seems hardly a suitable term to apply to the whole of Israel, to those who came and those who stayed behind alike, especially as the latter, a few verses on, are treated with mockery and rebuke. Would it be possible to follow a hint of Budde's (p. 103) and attempt to correct this verse from 11ᵇ, which we found to be a corrupt repetition of the words before us? We might read לִשְׂעָרִים for לְאַדִּירִים; the change would be a slight one. עם must go with יהוה.

14. מִנִּי אפרים שרשם בעמלק] tr. *from Ephraim (came they) whose root is in Amalek;* i. e. those Ephraimites who had their centre in the mountains of Amalek, 12, 15. For this metaph. use of שׁרשׁ cf. Is. 27, 6. Job 5, 3. ψ. 80, 10. The omission of the relative is harsh, especially when the relative includes the subject, Ew., § 333ᵇ. He compares Is. 48, 14. 21. Aug. Müller (p. 17 *n.*) distrusts מני as it stands, and thinks that the plur. suff. in שרשם points to the י in מני as a trace of what must have been originally a plur. ending. But it is difficult to suggest any correction of מני.

אַחֲרֶיךָ וגו׳] tr. *(marching) behind thee, Benjamin, with thy tribesmen.* עממיך uncontracted form, cf. Neh. 9, 22. 24 (עממי). Cf. v. 15 חקקי. *Out of Machir came down the leaders.* Machir was the eldest son of Manasseh, and the father of Gilead, Num. 27, 1. Hence the name might stand for the Manassites who dwelt in the districts of Gilead and Bashan on the E. of Jordan. See Num. 32, 39 J. Dt. 3, 15. Josh. 17, 1. 5. But on account of v. 17 Machir must also stand for the western Manassites.

מחקקים] Poel ptcp. of חקק ; cf. Gen. 49, 10. Dt. 33, 21. Is. 33, 22. Tr. *leaders;* cf. *v.* 9 *n.*

. . . *those who march with the marshal's staff.* For משך see on 4, 6. For the ספר in military sense see 2 K. 25, 19. ‖ Jer. 52, 25; cf. 2 C. 26, 11. For the שבט cf. Gen. 49, 10 and illustrate from Num. 21, 18. ψ. 60, 9. The ב here is that of concomitance. Cf. Gen. 32, 11 במקלי.

For Versions see p. 53.

15. ′ושׂרי ביששכר וגו] The first word is pointed with what looks like a suffix; but 'my princes in Issachar' does not give a suitable sense. Ges.-Kautzsch § 87. 1. c give it a doubtful place among such rare forms of the plural as ? חלוני, חשופי, חורי Is. 20, 4. It is safer to follow Pesh. Targ., and read וְשָׂרֵי Ber., Müller, Budde. For constr. st. before a prep. cf. ישבי על מדין *v.* 10 and note. But the text does not run very smoothly. Budde proposes ספרו שרי ביששכר עם דבורה *count (if you can) the princes in Issachar, Deborah's tribe.* Müller thinks that as Issachar is here classed with Deborah, so Barak's tribe (which he takes to be Naphtali) ought to be mentioned here. A correction of the same kind was suggested long ago by Meier (p. 44), who would substitute for the six letters ויששכר the same number in the word ודבורה, supposing that an old error was responsible for the change of name. But it is impossible to feel certain about any of these proposals.

′ויש׳ כן ב] To make the expression complete a כ should be prefixed to the first term of the comparison, e. g. ψ. 127, 4. Joel 2, 4; but in brief, poetic style it is sufficient to attach כן to the second proposition. Ew. § 360 a.

ברגליו] according to prevailing usage must mean 'at his feet,' i.e. as we should say, 'at his heels,' following him; cf. 4, 10. 8, 5. Ex. 20, 8 etc. (9 times). So tr. *into the valley they (Issachar) rushed forth behind him.* It might mean *on his feet* as in Num. 20, 19. Dt. 2, 28. 2 S. 2, 18. Am. 2, 15 (all); 'into the valley he rushed on his feet,' Ewald; but there would be no particular force in such an expression. Or again, 'he was driven by his feet' as Job 18, 8 כי שלח ברשת ברגליו ' *by his feet.*' The first way of taking the word is the best.

At the streams of Reuben there are great resolves ! but no deeds.

פְּלַגּוֹת] The plur. in fem. form only here, *v.* 16, and Job
20, 17. The sing. would be פְּלַג (usually פֶּלֶג), cf. נֶבֶר, שְׂעָר, נֶטַע,
רַע. It = *streams;* but Versions take it to mean *divisions.*
LXX. μερίδας B. διαιρέσεις A. Luc. Vulg., diviso contra se
Ruben. But Pesh. ܠܦܘܠܓܐ.

חִקְקֵי for וְחִקְקִי] rare shortening of *ŭ* into *ĭ;* cf. Is. 10, 1.
Ges. § 93. 1. 7.

16. מִשְׁפְּתַיִם] The root שפת = *put, place,* e. g. 2 K. 4, 38.
'put on.' Ezek. 24, 3. In Is. 26, 12. ψ. 22, 16 the meaning
is slightly extended. Accordingly מִשׁ means 'the place
where (flocks) are put.' It occurs again only in Gen. 49, 14.
It is dual, because folds were divided into two, cf. גררים Josh.
15, 36. Ewald, § 180 a, *doppelhürde.* Stade, § 340 b, classes it
with words which denote things that exist in pairs. The
word שפתים occurs in ψ. 68, 14=*folds*, and in Ezek. 40, 43 is
rendered *hooks*, but according to some ancient Versions *ledges*,
R.V.M., Cornill alters punctuation.

LXX. here διγομίας B. Μοσφαιθάμ A. Luc. Syr.-Hex. κλήρων
'A. (LXX. Gen. 49, 14). μεταιχμίων Σ. Vulg., inter terminos ;
Pesh. ܚܣܝܠ ܘܬܗ, both as in Gen. l. c.

Stade, *Geschichte,* i. p. 151, remarks that already at the time
of this Song Reuben had lost political importance; he preferred an easy agricultural life to taking part in the progress
of the nation.

לִפְלַגּוֹת] For ל of place, cf. *v.* 17 לחוף. ψ. 9, 5.

In the application of his stichical scheme (see p. 26) to this
verse, Aug. Müller is led to strike out clause [b], as a two-
membered verse is required. There can be little doubt that
these words are a corrupt repetition of 15[b]; so Reuss, 'after
the emphatic question למה וגו' they are dull and disturbing.'
Müller considers that חקרי is the original form which stood in
v. 15; the change, like that of בפ into לפ, was introduced
merely to make the repetition of the clause less obvious.

17. גִּלְעָד ... שכן] The earliest Israelite settlement in
East Jordan was in the land of Gilead. Reuben and Gad
settled there; and it appears from this verse that the latter

tribe was known in early times as Gilead after the name of its
territory. Stade, *Gesch.*, p. 148. The Pesh. has ــــ for גלעד.

בעבר הירדן] Cf. 10, 8. Josh. 2, 10. 7, 7. 9, 10 etc. The
expression denotes East Palestine, and implies that the author
was resident in West Palestine. So in the Pent. See Prof.
Driver's Article in *Expositor*, May, 1892, pp. 338 f.

ודן למה יגור אניות] For accus. of place after יגור, cf. Is.
33, 14. ψ. 5, 5.

It is difficult to suppose that Dan occupied the country
S.W. of Ephraim as far as the coast, since it is expressly said
in 1, 34 that the Amorites forced the Danites into the hill-
country, and would not suffer them to go down to the valley.
In Josh. 19, 46 the territory of Dan is said to have extended
to Joppa; but this is late, and comes from P. Thus our
passage is at variance with 1, 34, and implies that Dan *did*
take possession of the coast, and apparently developed into a
seafaring people. Against this we must set the northern
situation of the events alluded to in the Song, the context in
which Dan is mentioned, and especially the fact that in later
times the tribe settled in the north (18, 27 ff.). Accordingly
there must be some error in the text; Budde (p. 16 *n.*) ingeniously suggests נאתיו for אניות. See also Stade, *Gesch.*,
p. 166. Kittel, *Geschichte der Hebräer*, ii. 1892, p. 65 *n.*

אשר ישב לחוף ימים] The *shore of seas* must be the
Mediterranean, cf. Gen. 49, 13, where the ref. is to Zebulun.

ימים] plur. of extension over space, cf. Gen. 1, 10.

מפרציו] ά. λ. The root = *to burst, break*; so the noun will =
places where (the coast) is broken, cracks or *breaks*. Illustr. from
Job 38, 10 ואשבר עליו חקי of the sea-coast. For the significance of
the expression see Prof. G. A. Smith, *Expositor*, Feb. 1892, p. 146.

On these tribes, cf. the statements in Gen. 49, 13-17.
Dt. 33, 18-24.

18. In 4, 6 the tribes of Zebulun and Naphtali form the
army of Barak.

19. מלכים] i. e. those who owned Sisera as their overlord;
cf. the gathering of kings against Israel in Josh. 10, 3. 11,
1-6. For the 'kings of Canaan' cf. Josh. 5, 1.

תיענך] The modern Ta'annuk. Mentioned again in 1, 27 among the towns still inhabited by Canaanites in spite of the efforts of Manasseh to drive them out. On the list of Thothmes III. it is named Taâanak. *Records of the Past*, new series, vol. v. p. 46.

מגדו] The modern el-Lejjûn, probably the *Legio* of Eusebius. See Robinson, *Bibl. Researches*, 3rd ed., vol. ii. pp. 328–330. Baed., pp. 229 f. Though the identification is not certain, yet it is favoured by the fact that Taanach and Megiddo are always mentioned side by side, e. g. 1, 27. Josh. 17, 11. They both had kings of their own, Josh. 12, 21, and in time belonged to the tribe of Manasseh, 1 C. 7, 29. El-Lejjûn lies about 4½ miles N. of Ta'annuk, and it is still watered by a perennial branch of the Mukatta' (Kishon); hence the expression ' waters of Megiddo.' The town lay on the edge of the plain of Esdraelon, the battle-ground of Palestine, and gave its name to the plain of Kishon, Zech. 12, 11. 2 C. 35, 32. In later times Megiddo was one of the towns fortified by Solomon (1 K. 4, 12. 9, 15); Ahaziah, king of Judah, died here, mortally wounded (2 K. 9, 27). But it was with the defeat and death of Josiah at the hand of Pharaoh-Necho that Megiddo became specially associated in the mind of posterity (2 K. 23, 29), and Har-Magedon is the mystic name for the scene of the ' war of the great day of God, the Almighty ' (Rev. 16, 16). Lejjûn is situated at the north end of the pass which leads from the Sharon into the plain of Esdraelon. Through this opening the armies of Thothmes III. must have found a passage to the Hittite frontier and the Euphrates, and the Assyrian hosts must have poured through the same outlet on their way to Philistia and Egypt. It is not surprising, then, that we find Megiddo mentioned under the name of *Magti* among the places in Palestine conquered by Thothmes III. (*Records of the Past*, new series, vol. v. p. 43), and appearing in Assyrian Inscriptions as *Ma-gi-du-u* or *Ma-ga-du-u* (Schrader, *Cun. Inscr. and the O. T.*, vol. i. p. 156). *The city of Magid[di] or Makida* also occurs in the Tel el-Amarna Inscriptions, Tabl. 110, l. 24, and 113, l. 11 (*Records etc.*, pp. 81, 82). See further, Prof. G. A. Smith, *Expositor*, Feb. 1892, pp. 151 f.

20. *The stars* . . . *fought;* a poetical way of describing a great storm which descended at the time of the battle, ' with a vast quantity of rain and hail,' according to Jos., *Ant.* v. 5. 4, ' and the wind blew the rain in the face of the Canaanites, and so darkened their eyes, their arrows and slings were of no advantage to them.' For other instances of the intervention of the powers of nature, see Josh. 10, 11 JE. 1 S. 7, 10. Cf. ψ. 18, 5. Gen. 35, 5. Jer. 23, 19.

עַם] In hostile sense, cf. Ex. 17, 8. Num. 20, 3. Is. 3, 14. 1 S. 17, 33.

21. גְּרָפֵם] â. λ. *Swept them away.* The root has this meaning in Arabic, e. g. جَرَفَ النَّاسَ كَجَرْفِ السَّيْلِ *it swept away men like the sweeping away of the torrent* (Lane). The two derivatives from this root in Hebrew are אֶגְרֹף and מַגְרֵפָה, Joel 1, 17. LXX. ἐξέσυρεν B. Θ. ἐξέβαλεν A. Luc. Syr.-Hex. Vulg., traxit cadavera eorum (גּוּפֵם).

נַחַל קְדוּמִים] The meaning is uncertain. It has been rendered (1) *torrent of ancient time.* LXX. χειμάρρους ἀρχαίων. Pesh. ܘܦܡ. ܣܠܠ. Targ. ' the torrent where the wonders and mighty deeds of old (לְקַדְמִים) were wrought for Israel.' (2) Taking ק in hostile sense, like קָדַם, *torrent of onsets.* So in Arabic=*praecessit, accessit;* in Conj. iv. اقدم *audaciter praecessit* in hostem. (3) It might = *the on-rushing torrent,* alluding to the rapid and swollen waters. This would be a legitimate development of the root-meaning, and on the whole is to be preferred.

Θ. χ'. καδησειμ, so Luc. Vulg., torrens Cadumim. 'A. χ'. καυσώνων (=קָדִים). Σ. ἀγίων φάραγξ (=קְדוּשִׁים).

תִּדְרְכִי נַפְשִׁי עֹז] *Step on, my soul, with strength.* עֹז is to be taken as an accus. of manner, used adverbially; cf. Mic. 2, 3 לֹא הִלְכוּ רוֹמָה. Is. 48, 25. 60, 14. Hos. 15, 5 נְדָבָה אֹהֲבֵם. Ew. § 279 c. LXX. καταπατήσει αὐτὸν ψυχή μου δυνατή. Vulg., conculca anima mea robustos ; Targ., taking עֹז as accus. of obj. Hence A.V.

These words come in parenthetically, and betray the excited feelings with which the poet follows the course of the victory. Aug. Müller (p. 15), however, will not allow that the clause has any right here. His scheme requires a four-membered

verse, accordingly he adopts the two clauses of *v.* 22 into *v* 21ᵇ,
and treats עז נפשי תדרכי as the torso of *v.* 23, of which the
second member has been lost. Thus he obtains his required
sequence of *stichoi* 2. 4. 2 in *vv.* 20–22. But the alteration is
unnecessary, unless one starts with an *à priori* scheme.

22. סוס] Cf. 4, 3. 13. 15. The Verss. misunderstand הלמו.
LXX. ἐνεποδίσθησαν B. = ἐνευροκοπήθησαν, which is read by some
codd. ἀπεκόπησαν A. Luc.(? הִלְּמוּ). Pesh.ܘܣ. Vulg., ceciderunt.

מדהרות ד'א'] *with the prancings, the prancings, of his
mighty ones.* For the emphasizing of the word by repeating
it, cf. Joel 4, 14. Ges. § 123. 3. The root דהר, not found in
Arab. or Aram., occurs again in this sense, Nah. 3, 2 סוס
דהר ומרכבה מרקדה. A derivative תדהר denotes a kind of tree,
Is. 41, 19. 60, 13.

LXX. σπουδῇ ἔσπευσαν ἰσχυροὶ αὐτοῦ B. (?=מהר). ᾽Αμμα-
δαρὼθ δυνατῶν A. Luc. Syr.-Hex. ἐφορμώντων ἡ εὐπρέπεια ᾽Α.
(?=הדרת). Pesh. ܡܥ ܣܘܡܟܐ ܦ܇ܣܠܠ =*groaning;* so Targ. Vulg.,
per praeceps ruentibus.

23. *Curse ye Meroz, said the angel of Jehovah.* The town
probably lay on the route of the flight, and refused to aid
the pursuers to follow up the victory. Similarly Succoth
and Penuel refused to help Gideon, 8, 5–9. Meroz is not
found again, and its situation is unknown.
Bertheau understands the מלאך י"ע to be Jehovah Himself,
revealing Himself under the form of an angel to individuals:
cf. 2, 1. The prophetess Deborah had heard the command,
and what she had learnt from Jehovah she makes known to
the people.

24. In effective contrast to the selfish lethargy of Meroz is
placed the courageous activity of Jael.

מנשים] For this use of מן, to express one out of a number,
cf. Gen. 3, 1. 14. Dt. 33, 24.
Women in the tent: cf. 4, 11. 8, 11. Jer. 35, 7. Bickell and
Müller strike out the words אשת חבר הקיני; they might have
crept in as a gloss from 4, 17. Müller will not admit a
three-membered verse; the omission seems desirable.

25. The construction of the verbs ἀσυνδέτως gives force and
vividness to the description; cf. ψ. 46, 7.

E

חמאה ... חלב] occur again in parallelism Dt. 32, 14.
חמ׳ = *curdled milk.* LXX. βούτυρον.

26. תשלחנה] The form is that of the impf. 3rd or 2nd
fem. plur. ; but neither of these would be possible here.
Some explain it as an instance of the *modus energicus*, ending
in *anna*, as in Arab. But the occurrence of this mood cannot
be established in Hebrew. So it is safer to treat the last
syllable as a suff., and point תִּשְׁלַחְנָּה, Stade, *Lehrb.*, § 870 c.
Ges., § 47. 33. Other instances of the same peculiarity are
Ex. 1, 10. Is. 27, 11. 28, 3. Ob. 13. Job 17, 16. In each
case the text must either be altered, or the termination
pointed as a suffix.

וימינה] See above, pp. 10, 14.

הלמות] Only here. The ending suggests an abstract
meaning ; it might, however, be used in concrete sense like
ממלכות, מסכנת. The absol. form would be הַלָּמוּת, like פַּלָּצוּת.
Stade, *Lehrb.*, § 304 d.

עמלים] appears to mean *workmen, labouring men.* In this
sense it only occurs again in Prov. 16, 26 נפש עמל עמלה לו.
It usually means 'one who endures trouble or hardship' Job
3, 20. 20, 22, and is especially common in Eccl., where it is
used participially, of 'plaguing oneself with all kinds of
trouble and vexation ;' 2, 18. 22. 3, 9. 4, 8. 9, 9 (all). Its
use in Eccl., however, may well be a later development of the
root, which originally was used of physical toil.

והלמה ... ומחצה וחלפה] Perfects with weak waw. This
idiom, which is rare in the earlier books, seems to have been
preferred by the poet to the prosaic impf. with waw conv.,
which is only found once in the Song (*v.* 28). The different
acts are represented, not as arising out of each other (וַ), but
as standing each on an independent ground of its own ; the
'narrative advances not by development but by *accretion.*'
Driver, *Tenses*, §§ 131, 132.

מחקה] only here.

חלף] is used in the O. T. to express a *passing* movement.
usually forcible or violent. So it means to *pass by*, with a

sweep), Hab. 1, 11. Is. 8, 8. 21, 1. Job 4, 15 etc.; *pass away*,
Is. 2, 18. ψ. 90, 5. 6. Job 9, 26 (hence = *to change*, ψ. 102, 27,
as in Arabic ; and regularly in Pi. and Hif.); *pass on*, 1 S. 10, 3;
pass over, transgress, Is. 24, 5. Here, *pass against*, so *strike
through*, as in Job 20, 24 קשׁת נחושׁה תחלפהו ; only in these two
places with the accus.

27. [כרע נפל שׁכב] For the asyndeta cf. Ex. 15, 9. Ges.
§ 154 n. 1 a. The words describe vividly the effects of the
shattering blow. Literally translated they denote the three
actions, 'he dropped on his knees, fell headlong, and lay
stretched on the ground.' כרע is used specially with ברכים
to express 'kneeling;' so 7, 5. 6. 1 K. 8, 54. 19, 18. 2 K. 1, 13.
Is. 45, 3 etc. For נפל cf. 1 S. 28, 20 ; and for שׁכב cf. Lam.
2, 21. 2 S. 13, 31.

[שׁדוד] *destroyed, shattered*, cf. Is. 33, 1. Jer. 4, 30.

The second בין רגליה כרע נפל is an otiose repetition of
the first clause, due to the carelessness of the copyist. So
Reuss, Müller. The Pesh. omits, and the first clause בין ... שׁכב
is wanting in 11 MSS. Kenn. and 6 de Rossi.

28. The last scene is a fine piece of dramatic irony. To make
the satire more poignant, the mother of Sisera is imagined to
be waiting for her son's return. Her bitter disappointment
is not described, but silently dwelt upon by satisfied vengeance.

[נשׁקפה] *looked forth*. The root = inclinavit ; so in Nif. = se
proclinavit. Ges. *Thes.* The Arab. ﺳﻘﻒ has the meaning of
being 'tall and bent.' Hence the word is used in Hebr. of
looking out from an upper window, 2 S. 6, 16. 2 K. 9, 30
(Hif.).

[ותיבב] Only here. The root ﺣﺐ is common in Syriac
and in the Targg., and is always used in Pael. It = *cry, sound*
(e.g. with a trumpet). Payne Smith, *Lex.* s.v., quotes Arab.
أبّ, but this is not given in Lane.

For the order, subject coming in second clause, cf. *v.* 20.

[אשׁנב] *lattice*. Again in Prov. 7, 6 in parallelism with חלן.
For the form with א prefixed cf. אשׁפר, אשׁכר, אזרח.

[בשׁשׁ] Pil. cf. בושׁ, cf. כונן, עורר. The meaning is properly
to disappoint by delay. Again in Ex. 32, 1.

E 2

אֶחֳרוּ for 'אָ [מ' אחרו וגו'] *Why linger the steps of his team?*
(Piel). So in Gen. 34, 19 אֶחֵר; cf. יְחַתְּמַנִי for 'יְחַ ψ. 51, 7. Ges.
§ 64. 3. 3. מרכב here used not of the chariot, but of the
chariot-horses.

29. 'חכמות ש] *Her wisest princesses.* For the comparative
degree expressed by the genitive cf. Is. 19, 11 חכמי יעצי פרעה.
Ezek. 28, 7. ψ. 45, 13. Ges. § 133. 3. 1.

תענינה] may be defectively written for תענינה, cf. תראינה
Mic. 7, 10. ותדלנה Ex. 2, 16; or it may be a sing. with the
suff. of the 3rd sing. fem. Ges. § 75 Anm. 1. 6. For a sing.
verb after a plural used collectively cf. Gen. 49, 22. Joel 1, 20.

30. 'רחם וגו'] *A maiden, two maidens, for every man.* רחם
in this sense only here in O. T. It occurs on the Moabite
Stone l. 17 רהמת. The Verss. connect with the meaning
to pity. LXX. οἰκτείρμων οἰκτειρήσει B. φιλιάζων φίλοις A.
Luc. Syr.-Hex.

'לראש ג] Cf. for this distributive sense לגלגלת in Ex. 16, 16.
['שלל צבעים וגו

> *a spoil of dyed garments for Sisera,*
> *a spoil of dyed garments, a broidered cloth,*
> *a dyed garment, two broidered cloths, for . . .*

The root צבע=*dip* (cf. טבע), *dye;* the verb occurs in the
Aramaic part of Daniel, 4, 12. 20. 22. 5, 21. A derivative is
צבוע *a hyena,* Jer. 12, 9. In Arab. ضبع.

For רקמה cf. ψ. 45, 15. Ezek. 16, 10. 13. 18. 27, 7. 16. 24.
רקם=*an embroiderer* Ex. 26, 36 etc.

לצוארי שלל] has been taken in various ways: (1) *for the
neck of the spoil,* i. e. for the plundered animals (cf. 8, 21. 26)
or maidens. This is unnatural, and supplies too much with
שלל. (2) changing לצוארי; *for the neck* (לצוארים) *as a spoil,*
Vulg., ad ornanda colla; or, *for my neck* (לצוארַי); or, *for his
neck* (Sisera's, לצואריו), LXX. Keil, etc. Studer takes שלל as a
perf. in pause, and translates *for my neck hath he plundered it.*
(3) taking 'ש as an adj. with participial meaning, *for the neck
of the spoil-takers.* Pesh. ܒܓܘܐ̈ܪ ܕܒܙܬܐ. This is contrary
to the usage of the language. (4) Ewald ingeniously emends
שגל i. e. *queen, consort:* ψ. 45. 10. Neh. 2, 6. In Aram., Dan.

5, 2. 3. 23. This title seems to have been used in N. Palestine (ψ. 45), and of Persian and Babylonian queens; and as this Song is N. Palestinian the word would be suitable enough. This correction has found favour with many modern scholars (Bertheau, Wellh., Stade, etc.). But it cannot be considered certain, owing to the general insecurity of the text of this verse. The words שלל צבעים look very much like a repetition of the same clause above, and צבע, which comes in very awkwardly, might have found its way into the sentence from the line above it, and the third שלל appears also to be a corrupt repetition; so that the most probable text of this verse is:

הלא ימצאו יחלקו שלל
רחם רחמתים לראש גבר
שלל צבעים לסיסרא
רקמה רקמתים לצוארָי:

Thus we arrive at something like order out of chaos; the four lines become well-balanced as to rhythm and thought; רחם רחמתים corresponds suitably to רקמה רקמתים; and the three different persons introduced by ל appear in uninterrupted order. Müller and Budde propose some correction of this kind.

31. The epilogue or conclusion, perhaps added later. *Thine enemies:* cf. ψ. 68, 2. 3. 92, 10 etc.

כצאת הש׳ בגב׳] The sun was mythologically regarded as a giant or hero, who went forth every morning to run his course, ψ. 19, 7.

Clause ʰ comes from the Redactor's hand. See p. 3.

A few further notes on the Versions, too extensive to be inserted in the commentary, must be appended.

14. מני אפרים ... מחקקים] LXX. ἐξ ἐμοῦ· Ἐφραὶμ ἐξερίζωσεν αὐτοὺς ἐν τῷ Ἀμαλήκ· ὀπίσω σου, Βενιαμείν, ἐν τοῖς λαοῖς σου· ἐν ἐμοὶ Μαχεὶρ κατέβησαν ἐξερευνῶντες Β. μου· λαὸς Ἐφραὶμ ἐτιμωρήσατο αὐτοὺς ἐν κοιλάδι (Θ. Syr.-Hex.) ἀδελφοῦ σου, Βενιαμείν, ἐν λαοῖς σου· ἐξ ἐμοῦ Μαχεὶρ κατέβησαν ἐξερυν-

νῶντες Α, reading בעמק אחיך. So Luc., but ἐτιμωρήσαντο. Σ.
has for ἀδ'. . . . σου, ἀκολουθήσω σοι, Βεν'., μετὰ τῶν λαῶν τῶν
περὶ σέ. For ἐξερ'., Ἀ. has ἀκριβασταί. Σ. ἐπιτάσσοντες. Pesh.,
as in *v.* 9, محبـمل, and confuses אחריך with אהבתך; so Arab.
Targ. makes אפרים=Joshua, and בנימין=Saul, and renders
מחקקים by בקרבא כד מרשמים מרשמים 'quasi signati in bello.' Vulg.
nearly as LXX. B.

ספר ... [ומזבולן] LXX. καὶ ἀπὸ Ζαβουλὼν ἕλκοντες ἐν
ῥάβδῳ διηγήσεως γραμματέως Β. κ'. ἐκ Ζ. Κύριος ἐπόλεμεί μοι
ἐν δυνατοῖς ἐκεῖθεν· ἐν σκήπτρῳ ἐνισχύοντος ἡγήσεως Α. Luc.
(aliter, ἐνισχύοντες ἐν σκήπτρῳ διηγήσεως). Σ. διδάσκοντες
μετὰ σκήπτρῳ διηγήσεως γρ'. Θ. ἐπισπώμενοι ἐν ῥ'. δ'. Pesh.
'those who write with the pen of the scribe;' so Targ. Vulg.,
qui exercitum ducerent ad bellandum.

15. LXX. καὶ ἀρχηγοὶ ἐν Ἰσσαχαρ μετὰ Δεββώρας καὶ Βαράκ·
οὕτως Βαρὰκ ἐν κοιλάσιν ἀπέστειλεν (שׁלּח) ἐν ποσὶν αὐτοῦ· εἰς
τὰς μερίδας Ῥουβὴν μεγάλοι ἐξικνούμενοι καρδίαν Β. ἐνισχύοντος ἡγήσεως (see last verse) ἐν Ἰσσαχὰρ μετὰ Δεββώρας·
ἐξαπέστειλεν πεζοὺς αὐτοῦ εἰς τὴν κοιλάδα· ἵνα σοι κατοικῇς
ἐμμέσω χειλέων ἐξέτεινεν τοῖς ποσὶν αὐτοῦ διαιρέσεις Ῥουβὴν
μεγάλοι ἀκριβασμοὶ καρδίας. Α. So Luc., but reads the middle
clause ἵνα [τί] σὺ κατοικεῖς ἐν μέσῳ χιλίων; ἐξέτεινεν ἐν τοῖς
ποσὶν αὐτοῦ ἐν διαιρέσεσιν. So Syr.-Hex., but διαιρέσει for
last word. The clause ἵνα ... χειλέων is introduced from *v.* 16,
and when it is removed there appear (in Α. Luc. Syr.-Hex.)
two versions of בעמק ... ברגליו, viz. [ἐν τῇ κοιλάδι (so some
MSS.)] ἐξαπέστειλεν πεζοὺς αὐτοῦ and εἰς τὴν κοιλάδα ἐξέτεινεν
τοῖς ποσὶν αὐτοῦ.

The Pesh. renders בעמק by حقّـهـحل (? בעמיו), otherwise it
nearly follows the M. T. The Vulg. has for the second clause,
et Barac vestigia sunt secuti.

As to the variations in Hebrew MSS., they are slight and
of little importance. The most interesting are the following:—

3. [אנכי ליהוה] om. 4 MSS. Kenn., 1 de Rossi.
7. [פרזון] 2 MSS. K., 1 de R. read פרזות.
13. [לאדירים עם] Some 14 codd. connect עם with
foll. clause, as LXX.; 8 codd. connect לאדירים עם יהוה.

15. חֲקֵקִי] 2 MSS. K., 2 de R. read חקרי.

27. בֵּין רגליה כרע נפל שכב] Wanting in 11 MSS. K.,
6 de R.

31. וְאָהֲבִיו] 2 MSS. K. ואהביך.

A few *general* remarks as to the character of the principal
Versions.

1. LXX. is, of course, the most valuable and important.
The difficulties and obscurities of the text naturally lead to a
great many misunderstandings. *a.* Cod. B. goes less astray
than any of the Gk. Verss., and represents the M. T. on the
whole very fairly. E. g. *vv.* 7. 8. 13. 15. 17. 28. Occasionally
it agrees with A. and Luc. *vv.* 9. 12 (in part). 21. 23 (in part);
rarely with Luc. against A. 10ᵇ. *β.* Cod. A. is very much
inferior to B. (*v.* 2ᵃ is an exception) and differs from it widely.
A. is often loose in translation (e. g. *v.* 10), and often is obliged
to transliterate, *vv.* 7. 16. 21. 22. As a rule A. goes with Lucian,
e. g. *vv.* 7. 8ᵇ. 11ᵃ. 12 (both having an addition to B. and M.T.).
14. 16. 26. The commonest combination is A. Luc. and Syro-
Hexapla, e. g. *vv.* 2ᵇ. 6ᵃ. 11ᵃ. 13. 15. 17. 25. 28. 29. 30. Occasionally A. differs from Luc. e. g. *vv.* 4 (in rend. of נם שמים
ונטפו). 11ᵇ.

2. The Peshitto is generally careful, and understands the
text sometimes remarkably well. As a rule it follows the
M. T., e. g. *vv.* 14. 15. 16. 21. 23. 26. 30. Occasionally it is
free, e. g. *v.* 13, and leaves out clauses, *vv.* 27. 29. In *v.* 8 it
agrees with LXX. A. Luc. as against B. It agrees with the
Vulg. in *vv.* 11. 15 (partly). 16. 21ᶜ.

3. The Vulgate as a rule is free in its renderings, e. g. *vv.*
8. 9. 11. 13. 22. 26 (end). Sometimes it agrees with the
M. T., e. g. *vv.* 14. 16. 23. 26ᵇ. 30, and with LXX. B. e. g.
vv. 4. 7.

4. The Targum hardly ever fails to misunderstand the natural
meaning of the text. It is often extravagantly paraphrastic,
e. g. 4, 4. 5, 3. 4. 5. 8. 16. 26. 31; sometimes explanatory,

e. g. *v.* 14 (אפרים = Joshua, בנימין = Saul).   The 'leaders,' ' mar-
shals,' etc. are all turned into Rabbis and Scribes, e. g. *vv.* 9.
10. 14 etc.   Sometimes it agrees with the Pesh., e. g. *vv.* 7ᵇ.
22ᵇ. 27ᶜ.   In *vv.* 11. 19. 21 it is suggestive.

5. The Arabic almost invariably follows the Pesh., e. g. *vv.*
2. 8. 9. 13. 14. 31 etc.

A brief note on the *Theology of the Song.*

The Song of Deborah can hardly be called a religious poem,
although it contains a religious element sufficiently well
marked to enable us to form some idea of the theological
conceptions of the time.   The most significant feature, theo-
logically, in the Song is the occurrence of the name Jehovah
(*vv.* 2. 3. 4. 5. 9. 11 *bis.* 13. 23 *ter.* 31), and Jehovah the God
of Israel (*vv.* 3. 5).   Two main results follow from this fact.
(1) That the name of Israel's God at this time was Jehovah
(Jahweh) shews the lasting effect of the great inaugural
work of Moses.   It was he who first brought Israel to
realize Jehovah as their God.   Israel and Jehovah were
henceforth inseparably connected, and the true religion was
based upon this relationship.   Accordingly the use of the
name Jehovah in the Song, the summons to praise Him and
acknowledge His sovereignty and powerful intervention,
represents a wide-spread conviction as to His Nature and the
reality of His Presence.   Israel first learnt the elements of
this religion at the time of the Exodus.   We have seen
reason to believe that the opening verses of the Song look
back upon that ' marching forth' of Jehovah which so im-
pressively revealed His special interest in Israel.   That eventful epoch had already settled down in the mind of the people
as their most cherished memory; they had already arrived at
the conviction that Jehovah was their ' God from the land of
Egypt' (Hos. 12, 9. 13,4).   (2) Secondly, Jehovah is the God
of Israel.   Underlying the Song we can trace the presence of
the belief in some sort of national life or national unity bound

up with the acknowledgment of Jehovah as the national God. Israel is the 'people of Jehovah' (*v.* 41), Israel's enemies are Jehovah's enemies (*v.* 31), He fights in the battles of Israel (*vv.* 13. 23), and it is in Israel that His 'righteous acts' are done (*v.* 11). The belief in Jehovah as a 'man of war' was most characteristic of the time—Ex. 15, 3. cf. Num. 21, 14 (JE) 'book of the wars of Jehovah,' 10, 35 (JE) 'Let Jehovah arise and let His enemies be scattered,' cf. Ex. 17, 8 (J). Jud. 7. Every revival of religion was brought about by a victorious war.

The Song reflects no doubt the higher faith and temper of the age, both of them in the early stages of their development, and it gives us the picture of a people acknowledging Jehovah as their God, and believing in the reality of His protection and assistance in their affairs. This common belief was the bond that united the varied policies and interests of the different tribes. Israel was gradually growing into a nation; and the one thing that made it possible for the loosely-banded clans to hold their own in the country which they had only partly conquered, and to win higher stages of political and religious life, was their common belief in Jehovah the God of Israel.

www.ingramcontent.com/pod-product-compliance
Lightning Source LLC
Chambersburg PA
CBHW021531090426
42739CB00007B/874